APR

W9-AAG-785

Protecting
Intellectual Freedom in Your
Public Library

DISCARD

Intellectual Freedom Front Lines

Protecting Intellectual Freedom in Your Academic Library: Scenarios from the Front Lines
by Barbara M. Jones

Protecting Intellectual Freedom in Your Public Library: Scenarios from the Front Lines
by June Pinnell-Stephens

Protecting Intellectual Freedom in Your School Library: Scenarios from the Front Lines
by Pat R. Scales

Protecting
Intellectual
Freedom in Your
Public Library
Scenarios from the Front Lines

June Pinnell-Stephens
For the Office for Intellectual Freedom

AMERICAN LIBRARY ASSOCIATION

Chicago   2012

June Pinnell-Stephens recently retired as collection services manager at the Fairbanks (Alaska) North Star Borough Public Library. A graduate of Pomona College (BA) and the University of Washington (MLS), she is a past president of the Alaska and Pacific Northwest library associations, was elected to the ALA Executive Board, and served four terms as president of the American Civil Liberties Union of Alaska, where she remains on the Board of Directors. She was awarded the Robert B. Downs Intellectual Freedom Award from the University of Illinois Graduate School of Library and Information Science in 2003 and the Roll of Honor Award from the Freedom to Read Foundation in 2004.

Sidebars on pp. 11–12, 34–35, 36, 45–47, 49, 55–56, 58, 65, 74–75, 95, 107–8, 113–14, 117–18, by Deborah Caldwell-Stone.

© 2012 by the American Library Association. Any claim of copyright is subject to applicable limitations and exceptions, such as rights of fair use and library copying pursuant to Sections 107 and 108 of the U.S. Copyright Act. No copyright is claimed for content in the public domain, such as works of the U.S. government.

Printed in the United States of America

16   15   14   13   12   5   4   3   2   1

Extensive effort has gone into ensuring the reliability of the information in this book; however, the publisher makes no warranty, express or implied, with respect to the material contained herein.

ISBNs: 978-0-8389-3583-5 (paper); 978-0-8389-9380-4 (PDF). For more information on digital formats, visit the ALA Store at alastore.ala.org and select eEditions.

Library of Congress Cataloging-in-Publication Data
Pinnell-Stephens, June.
    Protecting intellectual freedom in your public library : scenarios from the front lines / June Pinnell-Stephens for the Office for Intellectual Freedom.
    p.   cm. —(Intellectual freedom front lines)
    Includes bibliographical references and index.
    ISBN 978-0-8389-3583-5 (alk. paper)
    1. Public libraries—Censorship—United States. 2. Public libraries—Censorship—United States—Case studies. 3. Intellectual freedom—United States. I. American Library Association. Office for Intellectual Freedom. II. Title.
    Z711.4.P56 2012
    025.2'130973—dc23   2011029691

♾ This paper meets the requirements of ANSI/NISO Z39.48-1992 (Permanence of Paper).

For Judith

ALA Editions purchases fund advocacy, awareness, and accreditation programs for library professionals worldwide.

Contents

Author's Note

My profound thanks to Deborah Caldwell-Stone and Christopher Rhodes for giving me this opportunity and helping me through it. Thanks, also, to Chris Finan, who told me the secret of getting the words on a page.

Throughout this book, I refer to policies from the Fairbanks (Alaska) North Star Borough Public Library for two reasons:

1. These policies reflect my views and best advice on the subject at hand, because I drafted them.
2. They also reflect the challenges, changes, and incidents I lived through in more than thirty years of defending intellectual freedom in libraries.

I am not an attorney, although I have had the benefit of advice from some of this country's preeminent First Amendment attorneys—always, always check with your library's attorney.

Anyone facing a challenge should not hesitate to contact the ALA Office for Intellectual Freedom at 800-545-2433, extension 4221, or oif@ala.org. Their help can range from finding a review to finding an attorney, and all of it can be as confidential as you want it to be. No one knows more about the problems we face, and their assistance can make the difference between making new friends for the library and losing your job.

Preface

The basis of intellectual freedom in libraries lies in the First Amendment to the U.S. Constitution: "Congress shall make no law . . . abridging the freedom of speech . . ." Over the years, courts have held that the right to speak is meaningless without the right to be heard, and so established a corollary right to receive speech. Since the public library is established by government specifically for the receipt of speech, the "quintessential locus of the receipt of information" according to the Third Circuit Court of Appeals, access to a public library is also a corollary First Amendment right.[1]

The First Amendment also contains a provision that guarantees the right "to petition the Government for a redress of grievances." It's this right that creates a dilemma for public libraries: we must protect both the right to read the book and the right to request that the book be removed.

While there are other rights that directly impact public libraries—the right to privacy in the Fourth Amendment, the right to due process in the Fifth Amendment, and the right to equal protection in the Fourteenth Amendment—it's the First Amendment that defines what we do and why—the essence of the library's role in a democracy.

Ours is a never-ending struggle, one we can't avoid by writing perfect policies or by refusing to add "controversial" items. It's a task that calls on us to look beyond our own preferences and prejudices, one that sometimes provokes personal attacks and confrontation; but the work of protecting the ideas entrusted to our care is the most profound responsibility of our profession.

---

1. *Kreimer v. Bureau of Police for the Town of Morristown*, 958 F.2d 1242 (3d Cir. 1992).

CHAPTER 1

Collection Development

Intellectual freedom cannot bring itself into existence. Librarians must apply the principles of intellectual freedom to activities undertaken daily—materials selection, reference service, reevaluation, protection of confidential patron information, and most important, collection building. It is in acquisition and its product, the collection, that intellectual freedom must be reflected.

—Judith F. Krug, *Intellectual Freedom Manual,* 7th ed., xvii

The foundation of building library collections and protecting them is having a collection development policy in place, one adopted by the governing body, so everyone knows how the library will select items and how it will handle challenges.

Because constitutional rights are implicated in both adding and removing material, all policies and procedures affecting the collection need to be content and viewpoint neutral, and they need to be applied equally. Also, the library must follow its adopted policies and procedures in all aspects of collection development—it's not enough just to have them in a policy manual someplace that no one can find and no one has read.

Not all of the cases that follow are the major community-wide incidents that generate hundreds of irate letters to the editor of the local newspaper or that result in heated testimony at a twelve-hour public hearing, but they do involve potential problems with various aspects of the collection.

CASE STUDY 1

A local resident, Jane, came across The Joy of Gay Sex *while browsing for a "safe" book about puberty for her twelve-year-old daughter. Jane demanded that the reference librarian, Susan, remove it immediately. Susan tried to explain that the library serves everyone in the community, but Jane remained adamant. Susan then gave Jane a copy of the collection development policy with the library's selection criteria and described how the library decided which books to buy. Jane was a bit calmer by then, but she still took the reconsideration form that Susan offered when the latter explained the procedure for registering a formal complaint.*

At this point, Jane has not filed a formal complaint, and that is how the story ends in the vast majority of incidents. The reason for the minimal instance of formal complaints is a staff that responds with respect, sympathy, and the ability to explain the basic selection process. For a detailed discussion of what should happen if the user does submit a formal reconsideration, please see chapter 5, "Challenges."

This case highlights the importance of having a comprehensive collection development policy in place. The collection development policy's most important job is to tell everyone—the public, the governing board, and the staff—how the library is developing the collection and why. Its importance for the public is to explain the values and procedures by which the staff will build the library collection and respond to complaints; for the governing board, it serves to gather the principles and policies they expect the library to follow when selecting and reconsidering material; and for the staff, it provides a blueprint for collection development as selectors change over time and a standard for all staff as they interact with the public.

The collection development policy must be in place before a major incident occurs. If it's not on the books in advance, the person filing the complaint will never believe it wasn't written just to frustrate her.

COLLECTION DEVELOPMENT POLICIES

The policy can be a short statement of goals, principles, and needs with collection management details in a separate document, or it can be comprehensive, with all collection-related material in one longer document. While each approach has its benefits, the longer version has the important bonus of preventing the details from getting lost.

Whichever approach works best for your library, it must cover the selection criteria and the intellectual freedom policies and procedures the library follows. It should also include

- a statement of the policy's purpose and intended audience
- the frequency of review by the governing body
- a general description of the collection and its goals
- a review of the users and how they can provide input
- an explanation of how your library manages its resources, either within a comprehensive document or as an attached document

In some cases, it is only the selection criteria and intellectual freedom statement that the governing board formally adopts, with the rest of the collection development policy residing in the library administration's control. Regardless, the collection development policy stands as the library's official document controlling the collection.

SELECTION

Selection is the heart of the collection development process, and the criteria your library adopts for guiding that process are critical, both for the library's success in serving the full spectrum of its users and for defending the collection when someone files a request for reconsideration.

There are occasional complaints stating that librarians are censors because they don't buy everything and allow their personal beliefs to determine what they do include in the collection. The classic analysis of this statement is Lester Asheim's article "Not Censorship but Selection," first published in 1953 and robustly pertinent today. These excerpts provide a brief synopsis:

> The major characteristic which makes for the all-important difference seems to be this: that the selector's approach is positive, while that of the censor is negative. This is more than a verbal quibble, it transforms the entire act and the steps included in it.

Collection Development Policy Elements

Introduction

- States purpose of the policy
- Describes what the policy covers
- Stipulates frequency of review by governing board

Collection Purpose or Mission

- Defines general goals of the library's collection
- Highlights priority areas of development, if applicable

User Needs

- Recognizes obligation to user-driven collection development
- Requires regular evaluation of user needs
- Emphasizes importance of user requests for additions

Intellectual Freedom

- Defines policies adopted by the governing body, e.g., Library Bill of Rights
- Requires neutrality of viewpoint and content in selection decisions
- Defines responsibility to provide all perspectives
- Defines parental responsibility for their own children's use of library resources
- Describes the reconsideration procedure

Selection

- Allows for individual professional judgment
- Describes review sources consulted

The selector says, if there is anything good in this book let us try to keep it; the censor says, if there is anything bad in this book, let us reject it. And since there is seldom a flawless work in any form, the censor's approach can destroy much that is worth saving.

Finally, the selector begins, ideally, with a presumption in favor of liberty of thought; the censor does not. The aim of the selector is to promote reading, not to inhibit it; to multiply the points of view which will find expression, not limit them; to be a channel for communication, not a bar against it. In a sense, perhaps, it could be said that the librarian is interfering with the freedom to read whenever he fails to make some book available. But viewed realistically, the librarian is promoting the freedom to read by making as accessible as possible as many things as he can, and his selection is more likely to be in the direction of stimulating controversy

- Reviews intellectual freedom principles that apply to selection
- Defines general criteria for selecting library materials
- Defines specific criteria for selecting library materials, e.g., information, opinion, or imagination
- Identifies any specific lists recognized by the library, e.g., best-seller lists from *Publisher's Weekly* or *The New York Times*

Collection Management

- Describes specific responsibilities and activities, e.g., discarding, processing, donations, and duplication
- Adds sections to cover problems as they arise, e.g., how to respond to questions about the books highlighted on the recently added or staff recommendations shelf

Collection Descriptions (optional section)

- Identifies specific parts of the collection in more depth, e.g., local history, periodicals, youth, and reference collections
- Describes the specific areas within each subcollection using a template, e.g., formats collected, any specific selection criteria, and management
- Identifies ephemeral collections, e.g., posters and sheet music

Appendixes

- Include any policies, forms, and material referred to in the policy, e.g., the Library Bill of Rights, suggestion forms, and the reconsideration form
- May mention policies or activities in process, e.g., disaster planning policy

and introducing innovation than in suppressing the new and perpetuating the stereotype. That is why he so often selects works which shock some people. The books which have something new to say are most likely to shock and consequently may not readily find another outlet through which to say it. The frequent forays of the censors against the libraries is heartening evidence that selection and censorship are different things.

Selection seeks to protect the right of the reader to read; censorship seeks to protect—not the right—but the reader himself from the fancied effects of his reading. The selector has faith in the intelligence of the reader; the censor has faith only in his own.

Selection is democratic while censorship is authoritarian, and in our democracy we have traditionally tended to put our trust in the selector rather than in the censor.[1]

The selection criteria should be broadly written to cover all material, regardless of source, and should be flexible enough to cover constantly changing technologies. The statement should also recognize the importance of professional judgment and the resources the staff may consult in the selection process.

It's important to remember that the library is defending the policy, not the specific book in a reconsideration request—if the book meets the library's adopted selection criteria, it deserves its place in the library.

The following sections demonstrate a general statement, followed by lists of general criteria and specific criteria for nonfiction and fiction material:

Selection of library materials, whether purchased or donated, is based upon the informational, educational, recreational, and professional needs of the community but is limited by factors such as budget, space, agreements with other libraries, and content of existing collections.

Every item must be considered in terms of its own excellence and the audience for whom it is intended. There is no single standard which can be applied in all acquisition decisions. Some materials may be judged primarily in terms of artistic merit, scholarship, or value as human documents; others are selected to satisfy the recreational or informational needs of the community. Materials are judged on total effect rather than specific illustrations, words, passages, or scenes which in themselves may be considered by some to be offensive.

A policy, however thorough, cannot replace the judgment of individual librarians, but only provides guidelines to assist them in choosing from the vast array of available materials. In selection, the librarian uses professional judgment and expertise, based on understanding of user needs and a knowledge of authors and publishers or producers. Reviews from professional, specialized, and general periodicals, in addition to standard lists of basic works, are also consulted. At times, the library staff may consult with others more knowledgeable in a specific subject for advice on developing that area.

Expanding areas of knowledge, changing social values, technological advances, and cultural differences require flexibility, open-mindedness, and responsiveness in the evaluation and reevaluation of all library materials. Material will not be excluded because of the origin, background, or views of the writer. In order to build collections of merit, whether purchased or donated, materials will be considered according to both general and specific criteria as listed below:

A. General Criteria for the Evaluation of Library Materials

- Reputation and/or significance of author, producer, performer, etc.;
- Suitability of subject and style for intended audience;
- Relation to existing collection and other material on the subject;
- Suitability of physical format for library use;
- Present and potential relevance to community needs;
- Appropriateness and effectiveness of medium to content;
- Insight into human and social conditions;
- Importance as a document of the times;
- Skill, competence, and purpose of author, producer, performer, etc.;
- Attention of critics, reviewers, and public; and/or
- Prizes, awards, or honors received.

B. Specific Criteria for the Evaluation of Works of Information and Opinion

- Authority of author;
- Comprehensiveness and depth of treatment;
- Objectivity and integrity;
- Clarity, accuracy, and logic of presentation;
- Representation of challenging works, including extreme and/or minority points of view; and/or
- Contribution to subject balance of the entire collection.

C. Specific Criteria for the Evaluation of Works of Imagination

- Representation of important movement, genre, trend, or national culture;
- Vitality and originality;
- Artistic expression, presentation, and experimentation;
- Sustained interest; and/or
- Effective characterization.

A reminder of professional responsibility in the task of selecting material for the library is in the interpretation of the Library Bill of Rights, "Diversity in Collection Development":

Intellectual freedom, the essence of equitable library services, provides for free access to all expressions of ideas through which any and all sides of a question, cause, or movement may be explored. Toleration is meaningless without tolerance for what some may consider detestable. Librarians cannot justly permit their own preferences to limit their degree of tolerance in collection development, because freedom is indivisible.

With a carefully crafted policy, expressive and flexible selection criteria, and a full recognition of the ethical responsibilities involved, the library should be in a strong position to develop and defend its collections.

INTELLECTUAL FREEDOM

This section of the collection development policy gathers all documents that have been adopted by the governing body and the procedures that the library uses when it receives a request to label, move, restrict, or remove an item. It is important to note that the ALA policies that are typically mentioned here, such as the Library Bill of Rights and its interpretations, change from private documents to official documents, as the governing body says: "We agree with these policies and adopt them as our legally guiding principles and procedures." The policy should cite these documents and include them in an appendix.

Important parts of this section tell the community that your library provides material to serve the entire spectrum of interests without personal prejudice; that the policy applies to minors; and that parents are responsible for their own children's use of library resources.

The intellection freedom section should also include the reconsideration procedure, so the public, staff, and governing body fully understand the steps that each must follow when the library receives a formal complaint. An additional benefit of including the procedure here is that this gives the library an argument for including the procedure in the code of local ordinances, which gives politicians a graceful way to avoid becoming embroiled in a major brouhaha, and prevents politicians who think removing the book is a good campaign issue from becoming embroiled, at least officially.

Whether or not the procedure enters the local code, the intellectual freedom section should include a statement that indicates the governing body is the last administrative remedy, and that anyone who wants to continue with the challenge must go to court.

Diversity in Collection Development
An Interpretation of the Library Bill of Rights

Collection development should reflect the philosophy inherent in Article II of the Library Bill of Rights: "Libraries should provide materials and information presenting all points of view on current and historical issues. Materials should not be proscribed or removed because of partisan or doctrinal disapproval." Library collections must represent the diversity of people and ideas in our society. There are many complex facets to any issue, and many contexts in which issues may be expressed, discussed, or interpreted. Librarians have an obligation to select and support access to materials and resources on all subjects that meet, as closely as possible, the needs, interests, and abilities of all persons in the community the library serves.

Librarians have a professional responsibility to be inclusive, not exclusive, in collection development and in the provision of interlibrary loan. Access to all materials and resources legally obtainable should be assured to the user, and policies should not unjustly exclude materials and resources even if they are offensive to the librarian or the user. This includes materials and resources that reflect a diversity of political, economic, religious, social, minority, and sexual issues. A balanced collection reflects a diversity of materials and resources, not an equality of numbers.

Collection development responsibilities include selecting materials and resources in different formats produced by independent, small and local producers as well as information resources from major producers and distributors. Materials and resources should represent the languages commonly used in the library's service community and should include formats that meet the needs of users with disabilities. Collection development and the selection of materials and resources should be done according to professional standards and established selection and review procedures. Librarians may seek to increase user awareness of materials and resources on various social concerns by many means, including, but not limited to, issuing lists of resources, arranging exhibits, and presenting programs.

Over time, individuals, groups, and entities have sought to limit the diversity of library collections. They cite a variety of reasons that include prejudicial language and ideas, political content, economic theory, social philosophies, religious beliefs, sexual content and expression, and other potentially controversial topics. Examples of such censorship may include removing or not selecting materials because they are considered by some as racist or sexist; not purchasing conservative religious materials; not selecting resources about or by minorities because it is thought these groups or interests are not represented in a community; or not providing information or materials from or about non-mainstream political entities. Librarians have a professional responsibility to be fair, just, and equitable and to give all library users equal protection in guarding against violation of the library patron's right to read, view, or listen to materials and resources protected by the First Amendment, no matter what the viewpoint of the author, creator, or selector. Librarians have an obligation to protect library collections from removal of materials and resources based on personal bias or prejudice.

Intellectual freedom, the essence of equitable library services, provides for free access to all expressions of ideas through which any and all sides of a question, cause, or movement may be explored. Toleration is meaningless without tolerance for what some may consider detestable. Librarians must not permit their own preferences to limit their degree of tolerance in collection development.

Adopted July 14, 1982, by the ALA Council; amended January 10, 1990; and July 2, 2008.

http://ifmanual.org/diversecollection

9

It is critical that your library follow its policies and procedures. Failure to do so may result in a court's finding the library guilty of removing material based on personal prejudice or belief, a case of "improper motivation," as noted in Board of Education, Island Trees Union Free School District No. 26 v. Pico, *457 U.S. 853 (1982).*

The following example illustrates a policy that includes both the intellectual freedom policy and the reconsideration procedure:

The Fairbanks North Star Borough Public Library subscribes to and supports the American Library Association's Library Bill of Rights and its interpretations (Appendix B), the Freedom to Read Statement (Appendix D), and Libraries: An American Value (Appendix F).

The library takes no sides on public issues and does not attempt to promote any beliefs or points of view through its collection. The library also does not endorse the opinions expressed in the materials held. The library recognizes its responsibility to provide materials presenting various and diverse points of view.

The standards stated in this policy will apply equally to the materials for children. The library believes that individuals may reject for themselves or their children materials which they find unsuitable. Parents are responsible for the use of library resources by their own children. Parents who wish to limit or restrict the use of the library by their children should personally oversee their selections.

Patrons concerned about material in the collection are welcome to discuss those concerns with a professional staff member. When patrons want the Selection Committee to reconsider items in the collection, they will be given the Request for Reconsideration form (see Appendix G), and informed of the reconsideration procedure. When the patron returns the completed form, the Collection Services Manager in the case of adult materials, the Youth Services Librarian in the case of youth materials, or the Circulation/Media Librarian in the case of audiovisual materials will read or examine the item in its entirety, gather any available reviews of the item, and report to the Selection Committee at its next scheduled meeting. The Committee will reevaluate the item in terms of the selection criteria, collection assessment data, collecting responsibilities, and the library's mission and roles statements. Committee members will vote by secret ballot, and the Library Director will communicate the Committee's decision to the individual who submitted the Request for Reconsideration.

If the patron wishes to appeal the decision of the Selection Committee, the Library Director will bring the complaint and supporting documentation to the Library Commission at the next regularly scheduled Commission meeting. In accordance with Borough Ordinance 2.32.041, five members of the Commission shall be required for a quorum and five affirmative votes shall be necessary to carry the question. The decision of the Commission shall be final. Further appeal must be referred to a court of competent jurisdiction within 30 days from the date the Commission mails its decision to the patron.

Board of Education v. Pico

The Public Library and the First Amendment

In 1976, members of the Island Trees School Board directed school officials to remove ten books from the school district's high school and junior high school libraries. The board members characterized the books as "anti-American, anti-Christian, anti-Semitic, and just plain filthy," and asserted that the books' removal was necessary to protect the district's students. Among the books ordered removed were Kurt Vonnegut Jr.'s *Slaughterhouse Five,* Langston Hughes's *Best Short Stories of Negro Writers, Go Ask Alice,* Alice Childress's *A Hero Ain't Nothin' but a Sandwich,* and Eldridge Cleaver's *Soul on Ice.*

A group of students led by Steven Pico filed a lawsuit to challenge the school board's actions, asserting that the school board's decision to remove the books violated students' First Amendment rights. The school board argued that both law and tradition had vested it with broad authority to control the materials available in the school library. The lawsuit eventually reached the United States Supreme Court.

In 1982, the Supreme Court decided *Board of Education, Island Trees Union Free School District No. 26 v. Pico.* The decision stands today as the principal legal authority addressing the censorship of library materials.

In its opinion, the court explicitly recognized a First Amendment right to receive information in the library, stating that "the right to receive ideas is a necessary predicate to the recipient's meaningful exercise of his own right of speech, press and political freedom," and identifying the library as the principal locus of the freedom "to inquire, to study and to evaluate. . . ."

The court then described the limits placed upon the board's authority to remove books from the library:

> Our Constitution does not permit the official suppression of ideas. Thus whether petitioners' removal of books from their school libraries denied respondents their First Amendment rights depends upon the motivation behind petitioners' actions.
>
> *If petitioners intended by their removal decision to deny respondents access to ideas with which petitioners disagreed, and if this intent was the decisive factor in petitioners' decision, then petitioners have exercised their discretion in violation of the Constitution.* (emphasis added)

Having established the standard for evaluating the student plaintiffs' claims, the court examined the evidence and found that there was a genuine issue as to whether the school board had violated the First Amendment rights of the plaintiffs. The court pointed to board members' statements that the removed books were "anti-American" and "offensive to . . . Americans in general" as proof of the board's improper motivation in removing the books from the library's collection.

The court said further proof of the board's bad intent could be found in the board's failure to use an established and unbiased procedure to review the challenged books. According to the record established in the case, the school board ignored its own established policy for reviewing controversial materials and disregarded the advice and information provided by the superintendent of schools, the librarians and teachers within the Island Trees School district, literary experts, and professional publications.

The court's opinion in *Pico* remains vital today. Courts uniformly apply the reasoning used in *Pico* to resolve censorship controversies in libraries; most recently, a federal district court in Wichita Falls, Texas, relied on *Pico* to determine whether the city council was motivated by a desire to suppress or eliminate disfavored ideas and viewpoints when it removed two books from the children's area of the local public library. In resolving the case in favor of the young library users whose First Amendment rights were violated by the removal of the two books, the court noted that the principles set forth in *Pico*—a school library case—have even greater force when applied to public libraries.

Books and other materials acquired by the public library through its established collection development policy are protected speech, and the library user's right to read and consult those materials is protected by the First Amendment. If a library's governing body undertakes to remove a book or other library materials from the library, it must do so using established and unbiased policies and procedures, and ensure that those policies and procedures are followed whenever an individual or group challenges library materials.

Additional Resources

Board of Education, Island Trees Union Free School District No. 26 v. Pico, 457 U.S. 853 (1982)

Sund v. City of Wichita Falls, 121 F. Supp. 2d 530 (N.D. Tex. 2000)

There is a sample reconsideration form and a letter responding to the person filing the complaint in chapter 5, "Challenges."

In the case of complaints, your library should be guided by the policies its governing board has adopted, in this case, the Library Bill of Rights interpretation "Access to Library Resources and Services Regardless of Sex, Gender Identity, Gender Expression, or Sexual Orientation":

> Library services, materials, and programs representing diverse points of view on sex, gender identity, gender expression, or sexual orientation should be considered for purchase and inclusion in library collections and programs. The Association affirms that attempts to proscribe or remove materials dealing with gay, lesbian, bisexual, and/or transgendered life without regard to the written, approved selection policy violate this tenet and constitute censorship.

COLLECTION MANAGEMENT

The rest of the cases in this section focus on collection management issues that can affect intellectual freedom. The library may never have to reply to a challenge based on these points, but they may be useful additions to the collection development policy, especially if they're on the books *before* a problem arises. Some of them may also help demonstrate the library's stewardship of the public's resources, which is a question that sometimes arises along with a major censorship incident.

CASE STUDY 2

The Rivertown Public Library has a collection of Christian books that it keeps in closed shelving in the staff area. They are mostly fiction in paperback format from religious publishers, such as Nelson and Bethany House, purchased from a local Christian bookstore. The library's selection committee had decided several years ago not to process them because they were viewed as inferior in "literary quality" compared to the general fiction collection and didn't really meet the library's selection criteria. Since they weren't fully processed, they weren't in the catalog, and users had to know about them by word of mouth and then ask for them at one of the public service desks. Rebecca finally got tired of never knowing which books were available and complained that she shouldn't be treated like a second-class citizen and neither should the books she likes.

Access to Library Resources and Services Regardless of Sex, Gender Identity, Gender Expression, or Sexual Orientation

An Interpretation of the Library Bill of Rights

American libraries exist and function within the context of a body of laws derived from the United States Constitution and the First Amendment. The Library Bill of Rights embodies the basic policies that guide libraries in the provision of services, materials, and programs.

In the preamble to its Library Bill of Rights, the American Library Association affirms that all libraries are forums for information and ideas. This concept of forum and its accompanying principle of inclusiveness pervade all six Articles of the Library Bill of Rights.

The American Library Association stringently and unequivocally maintains that libraries and librarians have an obligation to resist efforts that systematically exclude materials dealing with any subject matter, including sex, gender identity, gender expression, or sexual orientation:

- Article I of the Library Bill of Rights states that "Materials should not be excluded because of the origin, background, or views of those contributing to their creation." The Association affirms that books and other materials coming from gay, lesbian, bisexual, and/or transgendered presses, gay, lesbian, bisexual, and/or transgendered authors or other creators, and materials regardless of format or services dealing with gay, lesbian, bisexual, and/or transgendered life are protected by the Library Bill of Rights. Librarians are obligated by the Library Bill of Rights to endeavor to select materials without regard to the sex, gender identity, or sexual orientation of their creators by using the criteria identified in their written, approved selection policies (ALA policy 53.1.5).

- Article II maintains that "Libraries should provide materials and information presenting all points of view on current and historical issues. Materials should not be proscribed or removed because of partisan or doctrinal disapproval." Library services, materials, and programs representing diverse points of view on sex, gender identity, gender expression, or sexual orientation should be considered for purchase and inclusion in library collections and programs (ALA policies 53.1.1, 53.1.9, and 53.1.11). The Association affirms that attempts to proscribe or remove materials dealing with gay, lesbian, bisexual, and/or transgendered life without regard to the written, approved selection policy violate this tenet and constitute censorship.

- Articles III and IV mandate that libraries "challenge censorship" and cooperate with those "resisting abridgement of free expression and free access to ideas."

- Article V holds that "A person's right to use a library should not be denied or abridged because of origin, age, background, or views." In the Library Bill of Rights and all its Interpretations, it is intended that: "origin" encompasses all the characteristics of individuals that are inherent in the circumstances of their birth; "age" encompasses all the characteristics of individuals that are inherent in their levels of development and maturity; "background" encompasses all the characteristics of individuals that are a result of their life experiences; and "views" encompasses all the opinions and beliefs held and expressed by individuals. Therefore, Article V of the Library Bill of Rights mandates that library services, materials, and programs be available to all members of the community the library serves, without regard to sex, gender identity, gender expression, or sexual orientation. This includes providing youth with comprehensive sex education literature (ALA policy 52.5.2).

- Article VI maintains that "Libraries which make exhibit spaces and meeting rooms available to the public they serve should make such facilities available on an equitable basis, regardless of the beliefs or affiliations of individuals or groups requesting their use." This protection extends to all groups and members of the community the library serves, without regard to sex, gender identity, gender expression, or sexual orientation.

The American Library Association holds that any attempt, be it legal or extra-legal, to regulate or suppress library services, materials, or programs must be resisted in order that protected expression is not abridged. Librarians have a professional obligation to ensure that all library users have free and equal access to the entire range of library services, materials, and programs. Therefore, the Association strongly opposes any effort to limit access to information and ideas. The Association also encourages librarians to proactively support the First Amendment rights of all library users, regardless of sex, gender identity, gender expression, or sexual orientation.

Adopted June 30, 1993, by the ALA Council; amended July 12, 2000; June 30, 2004; and July 2, 2008.

http://ifmanual.org/accesslibrary

Collection Management Issues

The "Collection Management" section gathers together all the details involved in selection, acquisitions, processing, and maintenance; it provides a task-, not principle-, oriented perspective.

Evaluation or Assessment Method

- Describes how the staff analyzes the collection
- Helps set goals for growth or changes

Cooperative Collection Development

- Lists any collection development–based agreements with other libraries
- Helps explain why the library may not collect certain types of material

Selection Responsibilities

- Describes selection duties assigned to the staff
- Indicates who actually makes the final selection decisions
- Explains the nature and scope of any regular staff meetings devoted to collection development issues

Collection Assessment and Other Duties

- Describes other collection-related activities that may be assigned to the staff, e.g., reviewing interlibrary loan requests and sorting donations

Acquisitions

- Describes where the library orders its material and why
- Indicates the circumstances that might require a different procedure

Processing and Cataloging

- Describes how material is cataloged and processed
- Explains which material is fully processed, e.g., items purchased with library funds

Discarding

- Describes which material may be removed from the collection, why, and who makes the decision
- Explains what happens to the discarded items

Replacements/Rebinding

- Describes how the staff decides which items should be replaced or rebound
- Indicates which material may receive special consideration, e.g., out-of-print titles about local history

Duplication of Materials

- Explains how selectors decide when to buy extra copies of a title, either for the main library or branches
- Indicates when duplicate copies might be appropriate in different places, e.g., adult and juvenile fiction collections for certain classics

Donations/Memorials

- Describes how selectors decide whether or not to add donations to the collection and what the library does with the items it doesn't add
- Explains that the library will not provide a monetary value for donations and why
- Describes the process for memorial donations

Local Authors Collection

- Explains how the library handles material published by local residents

New Books/Staff Picks

- Describes the nature of material included in special display shelving
- Explains that displaying these items does not denote endorsement

Collection Maintenance

- Describes the extent to which the library will undertake preservation or conservation of library material
- Mentions any plans the library may have for disaster preparedness or other maintenance issues

There are many ways to keep books away from the readers who want them, and putting them in staff-only shelves with no record in the catalog is one of them. The fact that users are asking for them in spite of this barrier is a clear indication that the library has failed to recognize its users' needs. Further, the barrier rests on a biased assessment: rejecting Christian fiction on the basis that it doesn't meet the library's selection criteria for literary quality makes it very difficult to justify purchasing multiple copies of some best-selling titles.

Another way to keep "controversial" material away from the user is for the cataloger or processor to select which items come out of the backlog based on personal beliefs. Many automated systems can now track a book's progress from order to circulation-ready item, and your library might want to include a monthly report that lists material spending a longer-than-average time in the processing area, just to check.

CASE STUDY 3

Dave just started a job as manager of a small branch library in the Big City Library System. As he settled in and explored the library, he found the shelves set aside for discards. He noticed that many of the items seemed to be in good shape and had fairly recent publication dates. Puzzled, he looked at them more closely and realized that all of them were "controversial." He hadn't been able to find a copy of the system's discard procedures, but he remembered an encouraging discussion about intellectual freedom with the system director in his interview and was surprised at what appeared to be "censorship by weeding."

In this case, Dave has exposed a way that some librarians quietly dispose of material which they may dislike or which they fear may become a target of controversy. All libraries need to evaluate their collections regularly, so they can free up valuable shelf space by removing items that are outdated, superseded, or badly worn. This practice is sound collection management and something few libraries get around to frequently enough.

However, when libraries remove items because of their "controversial" content, they are practicing censorship, not collection management.

Further, removing material without following the library's reconsideration procedure, as above, may invite legal problems because of "improper motivation."

Evaluating Library Collections
An Interpretation of the Library Bill of Rights

The continuous review of library materials is necessary as a means of maintaining an active library collection of current interest to users. In the process, materials may be added and physically deteriorated or obsolete materials may be replaced or removed in accordance with the collection maintenance policy of a given library and the needs of the community it serves. Continued evaluation is closely related to the goals and responsibilities of each library and is a valuable tool of collection development. This procedure is not to be used as a convenient means to remove materials that might be viewed as controversial or objectionable. Such abuse of the evaluation function violates the principles of intellectual freedom and is in opposition to the Preamble and Articles I and II of the Library Bill of Rights, which state:

> The American Library Association affirms that all libraries are forums for information and ideas, and that the following basic policies should guide their services.
>
> 1. Books and other library resources should be provided for the interest, information, and enlightenment of all people of the community the library serves. Materials should not be excluded because of the origin, background, or views of those contributing to their creation.
>
> 2. Libraries should provide materials and information presenting all points of view on current and historical issues. Materials should not be proscribed or removed because of partisan or doctrinal disapproval.

The American Library Association opposes internal censorship and strongly urges that libraries adopt guidelines setting forth the positive purposes and principles of evaluation of materials in library collections.

Adopted February 2, 1973, by the ALA Council; amended July 1, 1981; and June 2, 2008.

http://ifmanual.org/evaluatinglibrary

The interpretation "Evaluating Library Collections" can help develop and explain weeding procedures to both the staff and the public.

CASE STUDY 4

For the last six months, Lakeside Township has been embroiled in a major controversy about a sex education title that discusses abortion in the high school library. Sally, the public library director, decided to make two copies of the book available there, so that the community could examine it, but no one had filed a complaint with her. Agnes, a member of the Keep Lakeside Township Clean coalition, a group that formed to get rid of the book, brought in a box of books and demanded that Sally add all of them to the collection. After examining each book, she decided to add only four of the eleven items, since the library already had two of them, and the others were either too old or too damaged. The KLTC coalition accused Sally of bias and censorship in a newspaper interview, because she didn't add all the books.

This situation may be uncomfortable, but if the library accedes to their request, it will be setting an unfortunate precedent and may find it difficult to refuse future requests, regardless of suitability. It's important to establish the policy that selectors will evaluate all material, regardless of the source, on the basis of their library's adopted selection criteria, and will handle materials according to the library's collection management policies and procedures. It's also important to be able to demonstrate that the library has material in the collection that represents the full spectrum of viewpoints, particularly in sensitive areas. See the interpretation "Diversity in Collection Development."

OTHER POTENTIAL COLLECTION-RELATED COMPLAINTS

The library won't buy the textbooks I need for my high school class.

There are so many school textbooks that your library may not have the space or the budget to collect them. Also, if the library participates in a cooperative collection development agreement, there may be a collecting priority statement that places responsibility for this material with the school district libraries.

I've been waiting for your books about tattoos for six months, and now I've found out they've all been stolen. Again. How long do I have to wait before you buy new copies?

Some books seem to walk out the door as soon as they're replaced. If the library decides it won't replace them at some point, it should probably have a statement justifying the decision on a management-directed, content-neutral basis. Otherwise, the practice could be used as another quiet way to get rid of "unacceptable" material, or the library could be accused of bias.

You spend all that taxpayer money with a company in NotYourState, not here in town.

I've included this item only because it's related to the collection. The library may want to have a statement in its policy that explains the discounts and time saved by dealing with a primary vendor, to prevent hearing this comment from the mayor.

You never have enough best sellers. Why don't you buy more copies so I don't have to wait so long?

For some titles, the library could never buy enough copies to fill the demand. Since this complaint surfaces fairly regularly, the collection management section should have a statement that describes how and when the library buys duplicate copies.

I've just written a wonderful history of my home town, back in NotYourState. I'll give you these four copies, and I can't wait to see them on the shelves.

Particularly with the advent of desktop publishing, many people are producing books. While your library wants to accommodate its local residents, it also doesn't want to accept material for the collection that doesn't meet the selection criteria. In this instance, the library may want to establish a special collection, one that appears in the catalog, so people can find it, but one that receives minimal processing. These items should be available somewhere in the library other than the main stacks, like a special collections area or display case.

Why don't you have any computer games I can check out? I can't afford to keep buying them.

Adding a new format of material to the collection is more complicated than the public realizes. Particularly with new electronic media, your library may need new shelving and processing supplies, in addition to new cataloging paths. Also, providing more than just a few items is important for an opening-day collection. Having a statement in the policy helps explain these decisions and gives them authority.

I found this DVD on the Staff Picks shelf. Why are you pushing this trash?

If your library has an area that displays new books or staff recommendations, it may receive complaints like this one. Including a statement reminding users that the library does not endorse the material in the collection can help answer this question. Also, the policy should include a specific statement that supports the staff's freedom to choose material based on their personal judgment. The staff should be alert to users who put their own choices in these areas in order to provoke a challenge by highlighting particularly graphic or explicit items.

QUESTIONS TO ASK

- Does the library have a collection development policy with selection criteria?
- Has the library board adopted the ALA Library Bill of Rights and its interpretations? Any other intellectual freedom policies or statements?
- Is there a reconsideration procedure?
- Is there a form available for a reconsideration request?
- Are these documents readily available to the public? How and where?
- Does the staff know about these policies and procedures?

NOTE

1. Lester Asheim, "Not Censorship but Selection," *Wilson Library Bulletin* 28 (September 1953): 63–67.

CHAPTER 2

Access to Library Resources

Most problems of access to library resources arise because libraries are trying to avoid controversy by restricting access to "objectionable" materials, either for all users or, more often, for minors. Restrictions may also be used to prevent children from getting library cards; from checking out a particular type of material, like DVDs; or from using the adult section. The restrictions may apply to those under eighteen years of age or some other, seemingly arbitrary age. However, the First Amendment doesn't have an age limit—it's a right, not a privilege, like a driver's license—and courts have held that minors do possess First Amendment rights.

As an example of just how important it is to allow access to the material users want, Judith Krug once related an incident she heard from Paula Johnson, an author of young adult books, at a conference.

Free Access to Libraries for Minors
An Interpretation of the Library Bill of Rights

Library policies and procedures that effectively deny minors equal and equitable access to all library resources and services available to other users violate the Library Bill of Rights. The American Library Association opposes all attempts to restrict access to library services, materials, and facilities based on the age of library users.

Article V of the Library Bill of Rights states, "A person's right to use a library should not be denied or abridged because of origin, age, background, or views." The "right to use a library" includes free access to, and unrestricted use of, all the services, materials, and facilities the library has to offer. Every restriction on access to, and use of, library resources, based solely on the chronological age, educational level, literacy skills, or legal emancipation of users violates Article V.

Libraries are charged with the mission of providing services and developing resources to meet the diverse information needs and interests of the communities they serve. Services, materials, and facilities that fulfill the needs and interests of library users at different stages in their personal development are a necessary part of library resources. The needs and interests of each library user, and resources appropriate to meet those needs and interests, must be determined on an individual basis. Librarians cannot predict what resources will best fulfill the needs and interests of any individual user based on a single criterion such as chronological age, educational level, literacy skills, or legal emancipation. Equitable access to all library resources and services shall not be abridged through restrictive scheduling or use policies.

Libraries should not limit the selection and development of library resources simply because minors will have access to them. Institutional self-censorship diminishes the credibility of the library in the community, and restricts access for all library users.

Children and young adults unquestionably possess First Amendment rights, including the right to receive information through the library in print, nonprint, or digital format. Constitutionally protected speech cannot be suppressed solely to protect children or young adults from ideas or images a legislative body believes to be unsuitable for them.[1] Librarians and library governing bodies should not resort to age restrictions in an effort to avoid actual or anticipated objections, because only a court of law can determine whether material is not constitutionally protected.

The mission, goals, and objectives of libraries cannot authorize librarians or library governing bodies to assume, abrogate, or overrule the rights and responsibilities of parents and guardians. As Libraries: An American Value states, "We affirm the responsibility and the right of all parents and guardians to guide their own children's use of the library and its resources and services." Librarians and library governing bodies cannot assume the role of parents or the functions of parental authority in the private relationship between parent and child. Librarians and governing bodies should maintain that only parents and guardians have the right and the responsibility to determine their children's—and only their children's—access to library resources.

Parents and guardians who do not want their children to have access to specific library services, materials, or facilities should so advise their children.

Lack of access to information can be harmful to minors. Librarians and library governing bodies have a public and professional obligation to ensure that all members of the community they serve have free, equal, and equitable access to the entire range of library resources regardless of content, approach, format, or amount of detail. This principle of library service applies equally to all users, minors as well as adults. Librarians and library governing bodies must uphold this principle in order to provide adequate and effective service to minors.

Note

1. See *Erznoznik v. City of Jacksonville,* 422 U.S. 205 (1975): "Speech that is neither obscene as to youths nor subject to some other legitimate proscription cannot be suppressed solely to protect the young from ideas or images that a legislative body thinks unsuitable for them. In most circumstances, the values protected by the First Amendment are no less applicable when government seeks to control the flow of information to minors." See also *Tinker v. Des Moines School Dist.,* 393 U.S. 503 (1969); *West Virginia Bd. of Ed. v. Barnette,* 319 U.S. 624 (1943); *AAMA v. Kendrick,* 244 F.3d 572 (7th Cir. 2001).

Adopted June 30, 1972, by the ALA Council; amended July 1, 1981; July 3, 1991; June 30, 2004; and July 2, 2008.

http://ifmanual.org/freeaccessminors

Paula had spent her early years in the segregated South, where she was not allowed to enter the "whites only" library, and where the "colored" library was anything but "equal." Then her family moved North. She went to the local library and half expected someone to prevent her from entering. Not only was she allowed to enter, but when she did, she saw books that reflected her face and her life. At that point she felt she belonged in this new community and was part of it.

CASE STUDY 1

Caitlin is a precocious reader and learner, and, in fifth grade, is doing school projects that students don't usually start until at least eighth grade. For her current project, she'd already gone through everything available in the children's section and had gone into the adult section for more material. When she tried to check the items out, however, the librarian told her that she couldn't have them unless a parent was with her, because she had a juvenile card. Caitlin tried to explain that her parents didn't get to leave work until after the library closed and her project was due the next day. The librarian said she was sorry, but Caitlin could not check out the books.

Many libraries still issue separate cards to adults and minors, often requiring an adult signature before issuing the minor's card. While this practice can lead to disappointment (and sometimes tears) when a class comes for a visit and there are a couple of children without cards, the problem in Caitlin's case is a largely outdated practice of not allowing children to check out adult books. An even more restrictive practice, fortunately not seen often any more, is refusing to allow children to even enter the adult section, much less check out books.

Many libraries also maintain separate juvenile and adult collections, sometimes because the buildings dictate the arrangement, but also because it can help the user find some types of material more easily, like picture books. Many also continue to issue separate cards, primarily to highlight parental responsibility for their children's library use. These practices are reasonable so long as libraries don't use them as a way to keep minors away from the rest, and probably the largest part, of the library. Your library's mission is to serve *everyone* in the community, and it can't accomplish that mission when it sets an arbitrary age limit as a barrier to that service. The library may also face a complaint of age discrimination, as one did for its "no children under age 8 without an adult allowed" policy.

The statement below by Bruce Ennis, former counsel to the Freedom to Read Foundation, discusses the First Amendment trouble you may face if you restrict access to your collections:

> Public libraries wisely leave the decision of reading material to the patrons—or their parents . . . Unless there is an applicable Harmful to Minors Act, *a policy of free access (limited only by parental decisions of appropriateness for very young children) provides the greatest insulation for the library from constitutional attack for restricting access to materials protected by the First Amendment.* Restrictions on access that are not based on valid administrative reasons (such as reasonable concerns about theft and vandalism) could be interpreted as restrictions based on disagreement by the government with the views expressed in the material. Thus, if government officials sought to remove or *restrict access* to a book on the ground that government officials opposed an idea in that book, the removal of the book clearly would violate the First Amendment.[1] (emphasis added)

CASE STUDY 2

The Midtown Library finally got fed up with its copies of computer games being stolen. A quick survey showed that only 41 percent of the titles were actually still in the collection. Worst of all were the Grand Theft Auto *titles—all of them were long overdue or just plain missing. When the new order of replacements came in, Linda, the library director, decided to put them "behind the desk," along with a few of the other frequent targets. Users would have to ask for them, but at least they'd have a chance of getting hold of them. When Edward, age fourteen, a regular user and avid gamer, discovered those games had been moved to a staff-only area, he complained that Linda was censoring them for their sexual content, because the rest of the games were for "little kids."*

There was a time when many, or perhaps most, libraries would have put any "adult" material in a restricted area, giving rise to catalog cards reading "For SEX, see Librarian." In this case, with the history of theft, Linda has a valid management reason for putting the games in a restricted area. She may also have a reference in her collection development policy about restricted collections.

Your library's rule should be that it's okay to put material in a restricted area if it's protecting the material from the user, but not if it's protecting the user from the material.

Restricted Access to Library Materials
An Interpretation of the Library Bill of Rights

Libraries are a traditional forum for the open exchange of information. Restricting access to library materials violates the basic tenets of the Library Bill of Rights.

Some libraries block access to certain materials by placing physical or virtual barriers between the user and those materials. For example, materials are sometimes placed in a "locked case," "adults only," "restricted shelf," or "high-demand" collection. Access to certain materials is sometimes restricted to protect them from theft or mutilation, or because of statutory authority or institutional mandate.

In some libraries, access is restricted based on computerized reading management programs that assign reading levels to books and/or users and limit choice to those materials on the program's reading list. Materials that are not on the reading management list have been removed from the collection in some school libraries. Organizing collections by reading management program level, ability, grade, or age level is another example of restricted access. Even though the chronological age or grade level of users is not representative of their information needs or total reading abilities, users may feel inhibited from selecting resources located in areas that do not correspond to their assigned characteristics.

Physical and virtual restrictions on access to library materials may generate psychological, service, or language skills barriers to access as well. Because restricted materials often deal with controversial, unusual, or sensitive subjects, having to ask a librarian or circulation clerk for access to them may be embarrassing or inhibiting for patrons desiring the materials. Even when a title is listed in the catalog with a reference to its restricted status, a barrier is placed between the patron and the publication. (See also "Labels and Rating Systems.") Because restricted materials often feature information that some people consider objectionable, potential library users may be predisposed to think of the materials as objectionable and, therefore, be reluctant to ask for access to them.

Although federal and state statutes require libraries that accept specific types of state and/or federal funding to install filters that limit access to Internet resources for minors and adults, filtering software applied to Internet stations in some libraries may prevent users from finding targeted categories of information, much of which is constitutionally protected. The use of Internet filters must be addressed through library policies and procedures to ensure that users receive information and that filters do not prevent users from exercising their First Amendment rights. Users have the right to unfiltered access to constitutionally protected information. (See also "Access to Electronic Information, Services, and Resources.")

Library policies that restrict access to materials for any reason must be carefully formulated and administered to ensure they do not violate established principles of intellectual freedom. This caution is reflected in ALA policies, such as "Evaluating Library Collections," "Free Access to Libraries for Minors," "Preservation Policy," and the ACRL "Code of Ethics for Special Collections Librarians."

Donated materials require special consideration. In keeping with the "Joint Statement on Access" of the American Library Association and Society of American Archivists, libraries should avoid accepting donor agreements or entering into contracts that impose permanent restrictions on special collections. As stated in the

"Joint Statement on Access," it is the responsibility of a library with such collections "to make available original research materials in its possession on equal terms of access."

A primary goal of the library profession is to facilitate access to all points of view on current and historical issues. All proposals for restricted access should be carefully scrutinized to ensure that the purpose is not to suppress a viewpoint or to place a barrier between users and content. Libraries must maintain policies and procedures that serve the diverse needs of their users and protect the First Amendment right to receive information.

Adopted February 2, 1973, by the ALA Council; amended July 1, 1981; July 3, 1991; July 12, 2000; June 30, 2004; January 28, 2009.

http://ifmanual.org/restrictedaccess

CASE STUDY 3

Sarah checked out a few DVDs, among them Obsessed. *Three days later, Emily, her mother, stormed into the library, incensed that her fifteen-year-old daughter had been allowed to check out an R-rated movie. Susan, the librarian, talked to Emily and explained the library's problem with using the MPAA film ratings or other labels for restricting access to any part of the library's collection. Emily didn't really agree with Susan, but she had calmed down by the time she left, saying she'd have a long talk with Sarah.*

This situation happens frequently, and the library needs to be prepared. The first issue is labels: they're okay if intended to get users to the right place, like classification numbers or a color dot to indicate a juvenile title in interfiled nonfiction collections. They are not okay, however, if they indicate a book that a minor may not check out or if they make the user reluctant to check it out, like a bright red SEX on the spine.

Rating systems are another problem. The most common assumption is that libraries use the Motion Picture Association of America, or MPAA, ratings to restrict access to minors, the way theaters do. Those ratings are the private system of the MPAA and have no standing in law. Further, the MPAA has said it will sue libraries that use its system to restrict access to anyone. Other systems attempt to prejudge interests and abilities by age and limit access on that basis. These systems, too, are a bad match for public libraries. Instead of these systems, your library should provide finding aids, recommended lists, and review sources to help users find material they find appropriate for themselves and their families.

CASE STUDY 4

Harriet, who had been the librarian at her small community library for many years, had adopted a practice of erasing the "vulgar" words in books when she came across them. She thought they simply weren't necessary and erasing them might prevent an unpleasant confrontation with an angry mother. She was, therefore, quite surprised when Sybil, a "new" user, was outraged that some of the words were missing from the copy of The Grapes of Wrath *that she'd checked out.*

No one is allowed to remove anything from library materials by erasing, cutting, or covering words or images that may be "controversial." Not only will it not prevent a challenge, but the library will be violating the author's copyright, which is illegal under federal law. On a slightly ironic note, covering the MPAA ratings on DVDs or films, even though the library may not use them to restrict access, is also a copyright violation.

QUESTIONS TO ASK

- Does the library issue separate cards to adults and minors?
- Does the library restrict minors from checking out adult material?
- Does the library use the MPAA film ratings in any policies or procedures?
- Are there any restricted collections, and, if so, what's in them and why?

NOTE

1. Bruce Ennis, "ALA Intellectual Freedom Policies and the First Amendment," www.ala.org/ala/aboutala/offices/oif/basics/alaintellectual.cfm (accessed July 1, 2009).

Labeling and Rating Systems
An Interpretation of the Library Bill of Rights

Libraries do not advocate the ideas found in their collections or in resources accessible through the library. The presence of books and other resources in a library does not indicate endorsement of their contents by the library. Likewise, providing access to digital information does not indicate endorsement or approval of that information by the library. Labeling and rating systems present distinct challenges to these intellectual freedom principles.

Labels on library materials may be viewpoint-neutral directional aids designed to save the time of users, or they may be attempts to prejudice or discourage users or restrict their access to materials. When labeling is an attempt to prejudice attitudes, it is a censor's tool. The American Library Association opposes labeling as a means of predisposing people's attitudes toward library materials.

Prejudicial labels are designed to restrict access, based on a value judgment that the content, language, or themes of the material, or the background or views of the creator(s) of the material, render it inappropriate or offensive for all or certain groups of users. The prejudicial label is used to warn, discourage, or prohibit users or certain groups of users from accessing the material. Such labels sometimes are used to place materials in restricted locations where access depends on staff intervention.

Viewpoint-neutral directional aids facilitate access by making it easier for users to locate materials. The materials are housed on open shelves and are equally accessible to all users, who may choose to consult or ignore the directional aids at their own discretion.

Directional aids can have the effect of prejudicial labels when their implementation becomes proscriptive rather than descriptive. When directional aids are used to forbid access or to suggest moral or doctrinal endorsement, the effect is the same as prejudicial labeling.

Many organizations use rating systems as a means of advising either their members or the general public regarding the organizations' opinions of the contents and suitability or appropriate age for use of certain books, films, recordings, Web sites, games, or other materials. The adoption, enforcement, or endorsement of any of these rating systems by a library violates the Library Bill of Rights. When requested, librarians should provide information about rating systems equitably, regardless of viewpoint.

Adopting such systems into law or library policy may be unconstitutional. If labeling or rating systems are mandated by law, the library should seek legal advice regarding the law's applicability to library operations.

Libraries sometimes acquire resources that include ratings as part of their packaging. Librarians should not endorse the inclusion of such rating systems; however, removing or destroying the ratings—if placed there by, or with permission of, the copyright holder—could constitute expurgation (see "Expurgation of Library Materials: An Interpretation of the Library Bill of Rights"). In addition, the inclusion of ratings on bibliographic records in library catalogs is a violation of the Library Bill of Rights.

Prejudicial labeling and ratings presuppose the existence of individuals or groups with wisdom to determine by authority what is appropriate or inappropriate for others. They presuppose that individuals must be directed in making up their minds about the ideas they examine. The American Library Association affirms the rights of individuals to form their own opinions about resources they choose to read or view.

Adopted July 13, 1951, by the ALA Council; amended June 25, 1971; July 1, 1981; June 26, 1990; January 19, 2005; July 15, 2009.

http://ifmanual.org/labelingrating

. . . .

Expurgation of Library Materials
An Interpretation of the Library Bill of Rights

Expurgating library materials is a violation of the Library Bill of Rights. Expurgation as defined by this interpretation includes any deletion, excision, alteration, editing, or obliteration of any part(s) of books or other library resources by the library, its agents, or its parent institution (if any) when done for the purposes of censorship. Such action stands in violation of Articles I, II, and III of the Library Bill of Rights, which state that "Materials should not be excluded because of the origin, background, or views of those contributing to their creation," that "Materials should not be proscribed or removed because of partisan or doctrinal disapproval," and that "Libraries should challenge censorship in the fulfillment of their responsibility to provide information and enlightenment."

The act of expurgation denies access to the complete work and the entire spectrum of ideas that the work is intended to express. This is censorship. Expurgation based on the premise that certain portions of a work may be harmful to minors is equally a violation of the Library Bill of Rights.

Expurgation without permission from the rights holder may violate the copyright provisions of the United States Code.

The decision of rights holders to alter or expurgate future versions of a work does not impose a duty on librarians to alter or expurgate earlier versions of a work. Librarians should resist such requests in the interest of historical preservation and opposition to censorship. Furthermore, librarians oppose expurgation of resources available through licensed collections. Expurgation of any library resource imposes a restriction, without regard to the rights and desires of all library users, by limiting access to ideas and information.

Adopted February 2, 1973, by the ALA Council; amended July 1, 1981; January 10, 1990; July 2, 2008.

http://ifmanual.org/expurgationlibrary

Sund v. City of Wichita Falls
Restricted Access in the Library

In 1999, a minister and his congregation sought to remove two picture books from the Wichita Falls Public Library. The books, *Daddy's Roommate* and *Heather Has Two Mommies,* were picture books about young children with gay and lesbian parents. Stating his belief that the books were inappropriate for children because of the books' "homosexual message," the minister had filed a formal challenge to the books with the library's advisory board. The board voted to retain the books in the collection after a reconsideration committee recommended that the books remain in the children's area of the library.

The Wichita Falls City Council subsequently passed a resolution that required the director of the Wichita Falls Public Library to remove a book from the children's section of the public library and place it in the adult area of the library if any 300 library cardholders signed a petition demanding the book's removal. This mechanism was immediately employed by the minister and his congregation to remove *Daddy's Roommate* and *Heather Has Two Mommies* from the children's room in the Wichita Falls Public Library.

City Council members who voted for the resolution said they adopted the resolution in order to keep the library comfortable for the public while minimizing any infringement on the rights of library users. They argued that no actual censorship resulted from the petition process because the books remained in the adult area of the library.

A group of citizens filed a lawsuit against the city of Wichita Falls in federal court, arguing that the act of moving the books from the children's area to the adult area of the library violated library users' First Amendment rights.

The federal district court agreed. In its opinion, *Sund v. City of Wichita Falls,* it held that the books could not be constitutionally removed from the children's room based on the petitioners' disagreement with the content and views expressed in those books. The court further held that the First Amendment was violated despite the fact that the books were not removed from the library entirely because "the burdens on Plaintiffs' First Amendment rights imposed by the Resolution are nonetheless constitutionally objectionable."

The court explained that the removal placed significant burdens on the ability of children and their parents to find the books while browsing in the children's section of the library:

> Even where a regulation does not silence speech altogether, the Supreme Court has given the most exacting scrutiny to regulations that suppress, disadvantage, or impose differential burdens upon speech because of its content . . . By authorizing the forced removal of children's books to the adult section of the Library, the Altman Resolution places a significant burden on Library patrons' ability to gain access to those books. Children searching specifically for those books in the designated children's areas of the Library will be unable to locate them. In addition, children who simply wish to browse in the children's sections of the Library will never find the censored books. Moreover, parents browsing the children's areas in search of books for their children will be unable to find the censored books.

The court permanently enjoined enforcement of the resolution and ordered the library to return *Daddy's Roommate* and *Heather Has Two Mommies* to the children's area of the Wichita Falls Public Library.

The decision in *Sund* demonstrates that a decision to restrict access to a book in the public library may violate the First Amendment if the intent is to prevent library users from gaining access to disfavored ideas or opinions. Such restrictions will be subject to strict review by the courts. Librarians should be cautious about imposing any restriction on library users' access that interferes with users' ability to freely browse, read, or use materials available in the library.

Additional Resources

Sund v. City of Wichita Falls, 121 F. Supp. 2d 530 (N.D. Tex. 2000)
Board of Education, Island Trees Union Free School District No. 26 v. Pico, 457 U.S. 853 (1982)

Libraries, Rating Systems, and the Law

Many persons believe that ratings affixed to movies, video games, and music recordings are "law," and that the library violates the law if it acquires and provides access to materials rated "mature," or for use by adults.

This perception is incorrect. The organizations that assign ratings, such as the Motion Picture Association of America (MPAA) and the Entertainment Software Ratings Board (ESRB) are not government agencies, nor are their activities sanctioned by local, state, or federal government. All are private trade associations whose members produce and distribute movies, games, and music. Each organization administers its ratings program as a benefit for its members, who want to give parents advance information about the movie, game, or song so the parents can decide whether or not a movie, game, or song is appropriate for their child.

An item's rating is meant to serve only as an informative advisory for parents. A rating such as the MPAA's "R" rating is not, and has never been, a legal determination that a particular motion picture is "obscene," or "obscene as to minors," or "harmful to minors." Only a court of law can make that determination.

Moreover, such rating systems are strictly voluntary. No law requires a filmmaker, game designer, or musician to submit their work for a rating, and no law requires a theater or retailer to follow the ratings guidelines when selling movie tickets, DVDs, games, or music. Those theater owners and dealers who enforce a rating system do so voluntarily to provide a service to parents.

Courts have invalidated laws and ordinances that enforce rating systems as a means of denying minors access to films, games, and other content, on the grounds that such restrictions violate minors' First Amendment rights. Among the cases are *Engdahl v. City of Kenosha,* which invalidated a Kenosha, Wisconsin, ordinance that used MPAA ratings to prohibit minors from seeing R-rated films; and *Motion Picture Association of America v. Specter,* which invalidated a Philadelphia criminal ordinance that penalized any theater allowing minors to view films rated "not suitable for children" by the MPAA. More recently, the Seventh Circuit Court of Appeals in Chicago and the Eighth Circuit Court of Appeals in St. Louis invalidated state and local ordinances that used the ESRB's private rating system to restrict minors' access to video games.

Librarians should not adopt policies that use private content rating systems to restrict library users' access to library materials. Instead, they should adopt and promote policies and practices that provide library users and parents with information to guide their choices and their children's choices and provide programming that equips young people with critical viewing and thinking skills that will enable them to make good judgments about the films, music, and games they view and use.

Additional Resources

Engdahl v. City of Kenosha, 317 F. Supp. 1133 (E.D. Wis. 1970)

Motion Picture Association of America v. Specter, 315 F. Supp. 824 (E.D. Pa. 1970)

American Amusement Mach. Association v. Kendrick, 244 F.3d 954 (7th Cir. 2001)

Interactive Digital Software Association v. St. Louis County, 329 F.3d 954 (8th Cir. 2003)

Access for Children and Young Adults to Nonprint Materials: An Interpretation of the Library Bill of Rights. American Library Association, 2004.

CHAPTER 3

Internet Resources

E very time libraries add a new material format to their resources, there seems to be a sudden flurry of complaints, particularly if the medium is visual. Those complaints reflect the fear that people have when faced with a technology they don't understand and with changes they can't control. They also focus on a perceived harm of exposing children to the new materials.

This reaction was certainly evident when public libraries introduced user access to the Internet. Although some people see the Internet as a cesspool of smut, research indicates that sexually explicit sites are not nearly so pervasive as the media would have the public believe. For example, a recent snapshot of the 50 most popular Internet sites includes only 2 sites that appear to be sexually explicit.

Aside from these considerations, the Internet presents a conundrum for libraries from a policy perspective. Unlike most of the other new

The Fifty Most Popular Websites May Be Surprising

The following list was taken from *Most Popular Websites'* Top Sites (http:mostpopularwebsites.net, March 27, 2010).

Yahoo!
www.yahoo.com

Google
www.google.com

YouTube
www.youtube.com

Windows Live
www.live.com

Microsoft Network (MSN)
www.msn.com

Myspace
www.myspace.com

Wikipedia
www.wikipedia.org

Facebook
www.facebook.com

Blogger.com
www.blogger.com

Yahoo! カテゴリ
www.yahoo.co.jp

Orkut
www.orkut.com

RapidShare
www.rapidshare.com

Baidu.com
www.baidu.com

Microsoft Corporation
www.microsoft.com

Google India
www.google.co.in

Google Deutschland
www.google.de

QQ.COM
www.qq.com

eBay
www.ebay.com

Hi5
www.hi5.com

Google France
www.google.fr

AOL
www.aol.com

Почта@Mail.ru
www.mail.ru

Google UK
www.google.co.uk

新浪新闻中心
www.sina.com.cn

FC2
www.fc2.com

media that have become part of a library's resources, the Internet isn't something the library can catalog, stamp, put on a shelf, and check out to a user. Does it fall under existing policies, or does the library need a separate policy just for the Internet? While many libraries depend on only a user policy that deals primarily with behavior, I recommend considering the Internet *as a whole* under the collection development policy. Libraries do not select Internet sites one at a time the way they do books—they acquire the Internet as a bundle, and, aside from software filters (more about them later), it's either there or it isn't. *The act of selection occurs when the library provides access to the Internet, and any challenges to its content must therefore be lodged against the entire resource.* I've discussed this approach at

Photobucket www.photobucket.com	**Яndex** www.yandex.ru
Google Brasil www.google.com.br	**Flickr** www.flickr.com
Amazon.com www.amazon.com	**Friendster** www.friendster.com
The Internet Movie Database www.imdb.com	**Skyrock** www.skyrock.com
V Kontakte www.vkontakte.ru	**Adult Friendfinder** www.adultfriendfinder.com
Google Italia www.google.it	**Go** www.go.com
Google España www.google.es	**Одноклассники.ru** www.odnoklassniki.ru
Google China www.google.cn	**Google México** www.google.com.mx
ImageShack www.imageshack.us	**BBC Newsline Ticker** www.bbc.co.uk
Youporn.com www.youporn.com	**Craigslist.org** www.craigslist.org
Wordpress.com www.wordpress.com	**Dailymotion** www.dailymotion.com
Google Japan www.google.co.jp	**Redtube.com** www.redtube.com
	CNN—Cable News Network www.cnn.com

greater length in the article "Lester Asheim in Cyberspace: A Tribute to Sound Reasoning."[1]

To help a newly elected mayor understand this prickly situation, our library sent him a position paper, which contained this explanation:

The library's Materials Selection Policy covers materials of all types and formats, including the Internet.

The Selection Criteria portion of the Materials Selection Policy states, "Expanding areas of knowledge, changing social values, *technological advances*, and cultural differences require flexibility, open-mindedness, and responsiveness in the evaluation and reevaluation of all library materials." Among the general and specific criteria for considering resources that apply to the Internet are:

- Appropriateness and effectiveness of medium to content
- Importance as a document of the times
- Insight into human and social conditions
- Present and potential relevance to community needs
- Relation to existing collection and other material on subject
- Comprehensiveness and depth of treatment
- Contribution of the work to balance the collection
- Representation of challenging works, including extreme and/or minority points of view

Another section of the Materials Selection Policy that applies to the Internet states that the library "subscribes to and supports the American Library Association Library Bill of Rights and its interpretations." The most recent of these interpretations is "Access to Digital Information, Services, and Networks" and states, "Libraries and librarians should not deny or limit access to information available via electronic resources because of its allegedly controversial content or because of the librarian's personal beliefs or fear of confrontation. Information retrieved or utilized electronically should be considered constitutionally protected unless determined otherwise by a court with appropriate jurisdiction."[2] (emphasis added)

By the way, I recommend that all libraries adopt the practice of informing newly elected officials about the sorts of situations that might escalate into a major brouhaha *before one occurs.* No elected official likes to be blind-sided by a controversy, and this "heads-up" may result in support for the library.

One of the library's most difficult problems is deciding what to do about

Pornography!!!

The real problem is that not all "pornography" is obscene, and only obscenity is illegal and not allowed in libraries. Further, only a court of law can decide which sexually explicit sites are obscene and which are merely "pornographic" and therefore protected under the First Amendment. Neither the library director, nor the police chief, nor the mayor has the authority to declare something obscene. People—including staff members—who find sites they believe to be obscene should rely on existing laws and report the sites to law enforcement personnel for investigation.

Even for the courts, finding a way to define obscenity took quite a while. Justice Potter Stewart once famously said that he couldn't define it, "but I know it when I see it."[3] In 1973 the U.S. Supreme Court decided *Miller v. California*

Access to Digital Information, Services, and Networks
An Interpretation of the Library Bill of Rights

Introduction

Freedom of expression is an inalienable human right and the foundation for self-government. Freedom of expression encompasses the freedom of speech and the corollary right to receive information.[1] Libraries and librarians protect and promote these rights regardless of the format or technology employed to create and disseminate information.

The American Library Association expresses the fundamental principles of librarianship in its "Code of Ethics" as well as in the Library Bill of Rights and its Interpretations. These principles guide librarians and library governing bodies in addressing issues of intellectual freedom that arise when the library provides access to digital information, services, and networks.

Libraries empower users by offering opportunities both for accessing the broadest range of information created by others and for creating and sharing information. Digital resources enhance the ability of libraries to fulfill this responsibility.

Libraries should regularly review issues arising from digital creation, distribution, retrieval, and archiving of information in the context of constitutional principles and ALA policies so that fundamental and traditional tenets of librarianship are upheld. Although digital information flows across boundaries and barriers despite attempts by individuals, governments, and private entities to channel or control it, many people lack access or capability to use or create digital information effectively.

In making decisions about how to offer access to digital information, services, and networks, each library should consider intellectual freedom principles in the context of its mission, goals, objectives, cooperative agreements, and the needs of the entire community it serves.

The Rights of Users

All library system and network policies, procedures, or regulations relating to digital information and services should be scrutinized for potential violation of user rights. User policies should be developed according to the policies and guidelines established by the American Library Association, including "Guidelines for the Development and Implementation of Policies, Regulations, and Procedures Affecting Access to Library Materials, Services, and Facilities."

Users' access should not be restricted or denied for expressing, receiving, creating, or participating in constitutionally protected speech. If access is restricted or denied for behavioral or other reasons, users should be provided due process, including, but not limited to, formal notice and a means of appeal.

Information retrieved, utilized, or created digitally is constitutionally protected unless determined otherwise by a court of competent jurisdiction. These rights extend to minors as well as adults ("Free Access to Libraries for Minors"; "Access to Resources and Services in the School Library Media Program"; "Access for Children and Young Adults to Nonprint Materials"; and "Minors and Internet Interactivity").[2]

Libraries should use technology to enhance, not deny, digital access. Users have the right to be free of unreasonable limitations or conditions set by libraries, librarians, system administrators, vendors, network service providers, or others. Contracts, agreements, and licenses entered into by libraries on behalf of their users should not violate this right. Libraries should provide library users the training and assistance necessary to find, evaluate, and use information effectively.

Users have both the right of confidentiality and the right of privacy. The library should uphold these rights by policy, procedure, and practice in accordance with "Privacy: An Interpretation of the Library Bill of Rights" and "Importance of Education to Intellectual Freedom: An Interpretation of the Library Bill of Rights."

Equity of Access

The digital environment provides expanding opportunities for everyone to participate in the information society, but individuals may face serious barriers to access.

Digital information, services, and networks provided directly or indirectly by the library should be equally, readily, and equitably accessible to all library users. American Library Association policies oppose the charging of user fees for the provision of information services by libraries that receive support from public funds (50.3 "Free Access to Information"; 53.1.14 "Economic Barriers to Information Access"; 60.1.1 "Diversity: Policy Objectives"; 61.1 "Library Services for the Poor: Policy Objectives"). All libraries should develop policies concerning access to digital information that are consistent with ALA's policies and guidelines, including "Economic Barriers to Information Access: An Interpretation of the Library Bill of Rights," "Guidelines for the Development and Implementation of Policies, Regulations, and Procedures Affecting Access to Library Materials, Services, and Facilities," and "Services to Persons with Disabilities: An Interpretation of the Library Bill of Rights."

Information Resources and Access

Libraries, acting within their mission and objectives, must support access to information on all subjects that serve the needs or interests of each user, regardless of the user's age or the content of the material. In order to preserve the cultural record and to prevent the loss of information, libraries may need to expand their selection or collection development policies to ensure preservation, in appropriate formats, of information obtained digitally. Libraries have an obligation to provide access to government information available in digital format.

Providing connections to global information, services, and networks is not the same as selecting and purchasing materials for a library collection. Libraries and librarians should not deny or limit access to digital information because of its allegedly controversial content or because of a librarian's personal beliefs or fear of confrontation. Furthermore, libraries and librarians should not deny access to digital information solely on the grounds that it is perceived to lack value. Parents and legal guardians who are concerned about their children's use of digital resources should provide guidance to their own children. Some information accessed digitally may not meet a library's selection or collection development policy. It is, therefore, left to each user to determine what is appropriate.

Publicly funded libraries have a legal obligation to provide access to constitutionally protected information. Federal, state, county, municipal, local, or library governing bodies sometimes require the use of Internet filters or other technological measures that block access to constitutionally protected information, contrary to the Library Bill of Rights (ALA Policy Manual, 53.1.17, "Resolution on the Use of Filtering Software in Libraries"). If a library uses a technological measure that blocks access to information, it should be set at the least restrictive level in order to minimize the blocking of constitutionally protected speech. Adults retain the right to access all constitutionally protected information and to ask for the technological measure to be disabled in a timely manner. Minors also retain the right to access constitutionally protected information and, at the minimum, have the right to ask the library or librarian to provide access to erroneously blocked information in a timely manner.

Libraries and librarians have an obligation to inform users of these rights and to provide the means to exercise these rights.[3]

Digital resources provide unprecedented opportunities to expand the scope of information available to users. Libraries and librarians should provide access to information presenting all points of view. The provision of access does not imply sponsorship or endorsement. These principles pertain to digital resources as much as they do to the more traditional sources of information in libraries ("Diversity in Collection Development").

Notes

1. *Martin v. Struthers,* 319 U.S. 141 (1943); *Lamont v. Postmaster General,* 381 U.S. 301 (1965); Susan Nevelow Mart, "The Right to Receive Information," 95 *Law Library Journal* 2 (2003).

2. *Tinker v. Des Moines Independent Community School District,* 393 U.S. 503 (1969); *Board of Education, Island Trees Union Free School District No. 26 v. Pico,* 457 U.S. 853 (1982); *American Amusement Machine Association v. Teri Kendrick,* 244 F.3d 954 (7th Cir. 2001); cert. denied, 534 U.S. 994 (2001).

3. "If some libraries do not have the capacity to unblock specific Web sites or to disable the filter or if it is shown that an adult user's election to view constitutionally protected Internet material is burdened in some other substantial way, that would be the subject for an as-applied challenge, not the facial challenge made in this case." *United States et al. v. American Library Association,* 539 U.S. 194 (2003) (Justice Kennedy, concurring).

Adopted January 24, 1996; amended January 19, 2005; and July 15, 2009, by the ALA Council.

http://ifmanual.org/accessdigital

and settled on a definition of obscenity. Many people confuse obscenity, which is not protected by the First Amendment, with pornography, which is; and although pornography is "in the eye of the beholder," only a court of law can determine if something is obscene. It wasn't until *Miller v. California*, involving a California mail-order business dealing in sexual material, that the courts developed the test they would apply when making that determination. In view of the perception that our policies promote access to obscenity on the Internet, we all need to understand how the courts define it.

The test consists of three parts:

1. The average person (not the most prudish, extreme, or devout, or the youngest), applying contemporary community standards (not some mid-1950s sitcom version of a Chamber of Commerce ideal), must find that the work, taken as a whole (not just an offensive bit), appeals to prurient interests (prurience is an unhealthy interest in sex, which implies there is also a healthy interest in sex);

2. It depicts or describes (text or images), in a patently offensive way, sexual conduct as defined by state law (the government needs to provide, in advance, notice of content that will not be allowed); and

3. The work, taken as a whole (again, not just an offensive bit), lacks serious literary, artistic, political, or scientific value.

Perhaps the most important word in this test is *AND*—all three parts must apply. The phrase "community standards," often cited by people who want to prevent access to sexually explicit material, appears only in the first part of the test; determination of redeeming value is made using a national standard. While it's important to understand the test, it's also critical to understand that librarians do not have the authority to make the determination of obscenity or to enforce the law prohibiting it.[4]

Defining Obscenity, Child Pornography, and "Indecent" Speech

The Supreme Court's decision in *Miller v. California* defines obscenity as materials that "depict or describe patently offensive hardcore sexual conduct," which "lacks serious literary, artistic, political, or scientific value." To determine if a particular work is obscene, a judge or jury must apply a three-part test, popularly called the *Miller* test, to the work in question. The questions the judge or jury must ask include

> Whether the average person, applying "contemporary community standards," would find the work, as a whole, appeals to prurient interests;

> Whether the work depicts or describes, in a patently offensive way, sexual conduct specifically defined by the applicable state law; and

> Whether the work, taken as a whole, lacks serious literary, artistic, political, or scientific value.

In a subsequent case, *Pope v. Illinois,* the Supreme Court clarified that the court's inquiry into a work's literary, artistic, political, or scientific value should be "whether a reasonable person would find such value in the material, taken as a whole."

The stringent standard established by the *Miller* test protects most sexually explicit expression. Materials many consider "pornographic" or "indecent" do not meet the standard for obscene material and are fully protected by the First Amendment. For example, in *Jenkins v. Georgia,* the Supreme Court emphasized that "nudity alone is not enough to make material legally obscene under the Miller standards."

Child pornography is the second category of sexually explicit material that may be banned or regulated by the state. In *New York v. Ferber,* the Supreme Court held that "works that *visually* depict sexual conduct by children below a specified age" are not protected by the First Amendment and need not meet the *Miller* test for obscenity in order to be banned, as the harm targeted by child pornography laws is the sexual abuse of the children used to create the images.

Not all depictions of children engaged in sexual conduct fall outside of the First Amendment. In *Ashcroft v. Free Speech Coalition,* the Supreme Court struck down portions of the Child Pornography Prevention Act (CPPA) that criminalized virtual images of child pornography that were created without the use of actual children. It held that such "virtual" child pornography—images created by an artist, or images of adults portraying children—are protected by the First Amendment if the images are not obscene under the *Miller* test. The court explained that laws banning actual child pornography are constitutional because the statutes target wrongful acts undertaken in the production of child pornography, rather than the content or ideas contained in child pornography. Because the CPPA criminalized works based on their content alone, it could not be upheld under the First Amendment.

In contrast to obscenity and child pornography, so-called "indecent speech"—colloquially called "pornography"—is fully protected by the First Amendment. In *Sable Communications of California, Inc. v. FCC,* the Supreme Court stated in no uncertain terms that "sexual expression which is indecent but not obscene is protected by the First Amendment." Over the years the Supreme Court has struck down laws regulating indecent speech made available through cable television, dial-a-porn phone services, and the Internet.

In *Ginsberg v. New York*, the Supreme Court ruled that federal and state legislators may regulate or restrict *minors'* access to constitutionally protected, sexually explicit speech. In upholding New York's law forbidding the sale of sexually explicit material to minors, the court reasoned that minors' First Amendment rights are more limited than adults, and that the government had a compelling interest in aiding parents' efforts to shield children from certain categories of indecent, sexually explicit speech. But the court warned that any such restrictions must be narrowly tailored so that adults' access to constitutionally protected, sexually explicit speech is not impaired.

As a result, Congress and state legislatures have passed laws restricting or regulating the dissemination of sexually explicit materials to minors. Under the standards set by *Ginsberg,* such laws, called "harmful to minors" or "obscene-as-to-minors" laws, must include the same safeguards for protected speech provided by the *Miller* test, only tailored to minors. Thus, such laws must protect minors' access to sexually themed speech that has serious literary, artistic, scientific, or political value for minors and may not restrict adults' rights to access non-obscene speech.

Courts will strike down "harmful to minors" laws when the law's definition of indecent speech sweeps too broadly or when the law's prohibitions unduly restrict adults' ability to access protected materials. For example, the Supreme Court's decision in *Reno v. ACLU* struck down portions of the Communications Decency Act, a law intended to restrict minors' access to "indecent speech" available over the Internet. The court objected to the law's vague and overly broad restrictions on Internet content available to minors, which imposed unconstitutional restrictions on adults' access to vast amounts of protected speech.

Libraries and librarians need to understand their state laws restricting access to obscenity, child pornography, and "harmful to minors" materials. Prohibitions on child pornography, as defined by the law, are absolute and apply in all circumstances. But restrictions and regulations applied to obscene or "harmful to minors" materials may or may not apply to materials held by libraries.

For example, many obscenity and "harmful to minors" laws only apply to commercial transactions involving the sale or rental of these materials, as in Colorado. Other states, recognizing the educational mission of schools and libraries, provide exemptions for schools and libraries that collect sexually explicit materials for education and research.

Illinois, for example, provides that it is an affirmative defense to the charge of disseminating obscenity if the dissemination is to institutions or individuals having scientific or other special justification for possession of such material. Illinois also provides that it is an affirmative defense to the charge of distributing "harmful to minors" materials if the institution is "a bona fide school, museum, or public library, or a person acting in the course of his or her employment as an employee or official of such organization or retail outlet affiliated with and serving the educational purpose of such organization." Wyoming simply states that the state's obscenity statute does not apply to bona fide school, college, university, museum, or public library activities or to persons engaged in those activities in the course of their employment with those organizations.

Additional Resources

Miller v. California, 413 U.S. 15 (1973)
Pope v. Illinois, 481 U.S. 497 (1987)
Jenkins v. Georgia, 418 U.S. 153 (1974)
New York v. Ferber, 458 U.S. 557 (1969)
Ashcroft v. Free Speech Coalition, 535 U.S. 234 (2002)
United States v. Williams, 553 U.S. 285 (2008)
Sable Communications of California, Inc. v. FCC, 492 U.S. 115 (1989)
Ginsberg v. New York, 390 U.S. 629 (1968)
Reno v. American Civil Liberties Union, 521 U.S. 844 (1997)
Colorado Revised Statutes 18-7-502 (2007)
Illinois Revised Statutes 720 ILCS 5/11-20, 720 ILCS 11-21 (2008)
Wyoming Statutes § 6-4-302

INTERNET USE POLICY (IUP)

All libraries that provide public access to the Internet should adopt an Internet use, or Internet safety, policy, and all that receive E-Rate funding from the federal government are required to have one. These policies are actually a combination of policy and procedure, and they are intended to govern all Internet use in the library. Some may be a very simple statement for small libraries with one or two computers, while some may have to describe use in different areas of the library or in branches of various sizes and configurations. In any case, all IUPs should contain these elements at the very least:

- notice that the library uses software filters (if it does) and instructions for disabling or unblocking them
- statement of user responsibilities and rights
- details for actual use, including time limits, reservations, etc.

The IUP on pages 50–52 demonstrates policies in a variety of circumstances, including a primary bank of public workstations; a children's area; a branch or small library; a bank of non-reserved, short-term use workstations; and use of a personal computer. Your library's IUP needs to cover all configurations of Internet access, so that users understand, in advance, the conditions of Internet use anywhere in the library, and so the library has a basis on which to restrict or deny access if a user violates the policy.

There is, as with all library resources, a question of First Amendment rights. If the library restricts access to constitutionally protected speech, it might face legal consequences. There has not, however, been a successful proceeding against a library because it does provide access to the Internet.

CASE STUDY 1

When Sandy arrived at the reference desk for her shift, she noticed a few of the "regulars" at the public Internet workstations. She was looking forward to the new computerized booking system but was nervous about the new Internet stations. All the new monitors were sitting on top of the desk, instead of being recessed below glass like the other stations, and they were still waiting for the privacy screens that at least cut down on what folks passing by could see. After a flurry of reference questions, Sandy found her next customer—an older man with a red face and a (maybe) fourth-grader tightly gripped in tow. "Uh-oh," she thought. This grandfather had

Liability for Minors' Internet Use
Kathleen R. v. City of Livermore

The library has computers linked to the Internet, which patrons of any age are free to use. Twelve-year-old Brandon went to the computers without [his mother's] knowledge and downloaded sexually explicit photos from the Internet onto a floppy disk that he brought to the library. [Brandon's mother] alleges that the photos Brandon obtained are harmful to minors and that some of them are obscene.

When Brandon's mother, Kathleen R., learned about Brandon's activities, she filed a lawsuit against the City of Livermore and its public library. She claimed the library should be legally liable for providing obscene pornography to her minor son, even though the library did not itself exhibit the materials or teach Brandon how to access them.

A California appellate court ordered her lawsuit dismissed. It identified two reasons for rejecting her claims:

- First, the Court held that Section 230 of the Telecommunications Act of 1996 provides libraries with immunity from lawsuits seeking to hold libraries liable for content provided by a third party and accessed through the Internet. The library was therefore entitled to immunity from Kathleen R.'s lawsuit. The court explained, "There is a crucial distinction between providing minors with harmful matter on the one hand, and maintaining computers where minors may obtain such matter, however easily, on the other."

- Second, Kathleen R. could not claim that the library had a policy of providing obscene pornography to minors simply by permitting minors to access the Internet without supervision. According to the court, "any such implication would be contrary to the library policy attached to the complaint, which among other things prohibits the use of computer resources for illegal purposes." It further noted that the library's policy warned users that controversial material is available on the Internet, that users who use the Internet do so at their own risk, and that the library does not supervise minors' use of the Internet.

The result in *Kathleen R. v. City of Livermore* emphasizes the importance of having a comprehensive Internet use policy for the library. Such policies should inform library users, in particular parents and their minor children, about the guidelines for using computers and the consequences if those procedures are not followed, and state that the child and child's parents are jointly responsible for the child's computer use. In addition, the policy should alert parents about the possibility of encountering controversial materials on the Internet and inform all users that computers are not to be used for illegal purposes, including accessing illegal materials on the Internet.

Additional Resources

Kathleen R. v. City of Livermore, 87 Cal. App. 4th 684 (2001)

Telecommunications Act of 1996, 47 U.S.C. § 230

Internet Use Policy

This sample Internet Use Policy or IUP from the Fairbanks (Alaska) North Star Borough Public Library demonstrates the scope of the detail that should be included. The IUP is actually more a set of procedures than a statement of policy, but libraries receiving E-Rate funds are required to have a document that describes how they comply with the filtering mandate, and the regulations call that document an IUP.

Filtering Software

- Filtering software is enabled on all public access to the Internet. If users want staff to disable the filtering software, they must agree to the library's regulations and may be asked to prove they are at least 17 years old.

- Filtering will not be disabled on any computers in the Children's Room or the children's area of the Branch library.

- Parents and legal guardians may request that staff disable the filtering software for their own children, as long as the parent or guardian remains at the library. Others who request unfiltered workstations are responsible for preventing access by anyone younger than 17 years old during their sessions.

All Workstations

- Users are responsible for what they choose to view on the Internet.

- Parents or legal guardians are responsible for determining the nature of their own children's use of the Internet, including the use of e-mail, chat rooms, or other direct electronic communication.

- Users are required to observe the library's Patron Conduct Policy when using the Internet. Copies are available upon request.

- All use of library Internet workstations is limited to lawful purposes. Users are required to observe all federal, state, and local laws that may govern use of the Internet. These laws include, but are not limited to, those that regulate distribution of obscenity, possession of child pornography, fraud, theft, libel, harassment, invasion of privacy, disclosure of information that identifies a minor, copyright or patent infringement, unauthorized access, and, for users younger than 17 years of age, access to material harmful to minors.

- Objections to the Internet as a library resource will be handled according to the library's Reconsideration of Library Materials procedure. Copies are available upon request.

- No more than two people may use a station at the same time.

- Charges for Internet printing are $0.50 per page for color prints (available only at the main library through the centralized printing system) or $0.10 per page for black and white prints.

Library Reserved Workstations

- Users must reserve a designated Internet station by using the PC Reservation system.

- Library cardholders are required to use their cards to make reservations. Internet-only cards are available for others. A person who forgets the library card may use an Internet-only card for a single reservation.

- Reserved sessions are available for the current day and for up to 7 days in advance.

- Reservations by telephone are not available.

- Sessions may be reserved for up to 55 minutes. Shorter sessions may be offered, depending on the reservation schedule for the day.

- Reservations will be held for 10 minutes after the session is scheduled to begin. After that time, the system will automatically make the session available to others.

- Users are limited to one session per day, regardless of the length of the session.

- Users must log in using their card number and PIN to register their sessions.

Library QuickNet Workstation

- QuickNet stations are available on a first-come, first-served basis.

- Users are limited to one 15-minute session when someone is waiting.

- Sessions automatically time out after 15 minutes.

- Users are encouraged to wait in the designated seating area for the next available workstation.

Library Children's Room Workstations

- All sites accessible on the Children's Room workstations will be selected by library staff.

- Users must sign up through the Children's Room desk to use the Children's Room Internet stations. Users who have not signed up will be required to give up their places if someone else reserves the workstation.

- Sessions are available on a first-come, first-served basis.

- Sessions may be reserved for 30 minutes.

- Users are limited to one 30-minute session per day.

Internet Use Policy, continued

Branch Library Workstations

- Users must sign up at the Desk to use the Internet workstations.

- Reserved sessions are available for the current day only.

- Sessions may be reserved for 1 hour or 30 minutes, beginning on the hour or the half-hour.

- Reservations will be held for 10 minutes after the session is scheduled to begin. After that time, the session will be available to others.

- Users are limited to one hour per day.

Internet Access with Personal Computers and Other Devices

- Patrons may access the Internet with their personal computers and other devices at both the Main and Branch libraries.

- Access with a network cable is available at designated locations in the Main library.

- Wireless cards and network cables are available for use in the Main library.

- Due to liability issues, library staff are not able to help you set up your computer to connect to the library's network.

- Use of the wireless network is at your own risk. The Library is not responsible for any damage that may occur to you, your computer, or your software while connected to the wireless network.

come to the library to help his granddaughter with her homework. As he'd walked to their assigned station, he'd seen some "unspeakable filth" on the screen at station #2 and wanted to know what she was going to do about it. She thanked him for his concern and asked if he'd please step away from the desk so they could discuss the library's policy.

Under these circumstances, it may be difficult to remember the library's policies and procedures, but they exist to handle moments precisely like this one. The staff must be able to explain the library's Internet use policy, which all users are expected to follow. The IUP should be part of the opening screen for each session, possibly with an acceptance click required before the session can start. It should also be posted in hard copy at each station, at any sign-up point, and at the reference desk.

Many of the problems with public Internet stations involve parents who are upset about what their children might see. The library's IUP needs to remind parents that they have to be responsible for their own children's use of all library resources, including the Internet—the library simply cannot do it for them. In this case, the library could demonstrate that it had taken several steps to minimize incidental exposure by using privacy screens, stations with recessed screens, and stations situated away from the main lines of traffic, all of which can be effective content- and viewpoint-neutral ways both to avoid exposure and to protect user privacy.

If the library uses software filters (again, more later), the Internet stations would probably not display most sexually explicit sites. If, however, an adult requests an unfiltered session, which is his right, explicit sites would still be accessible, so the library needs to be prepared to handle possible complaints. In many instances, a user may complain about something she thinks is truly obscene. But unless a staff member actually sees a particular site, there's no way to tell if the content might warrant further action by the library, like child pornography. The user, however, can always contact legal authorities independently.

CASE STUDY 2

Robert runs a small public library in a small town in a rural part of the state. The library recently installed three public-access Internet stations after waiting for more than a year to get everything in place—wiring, furniture, and, of course, funding. Since the library is part of a regional system, he didn't have to worry about developing policies or, most important, whether or not to filter—those decisions were made by the folks at system headquarters. Robert was actually glad they decided to install software filters, partly because he didn't want to have to explain to Mommy and Daddy why little Susie saw some nasty pictures, but mostly because he couldn't afford to lose his library's share of E-Rate money from the federal government.

One thing was starting to bother him, though. He went to the library association conference and heard a panel discuss the different ways that libraries handle problems with filters. One of those problems was when or how or whether to disable the filter or unblock a site, as well as the possible consequences if a library didn't—or wouldn't— make unfiltered access available to an adult and do it quickly. Nobody had asked him to disable the filter yet, but he was concerned about the system's procedure, which required him to send the request to headquarters and wait until the director made a decision. He'd heard that some of the other librarians in the system had waited more than a week for an answer and that most of the answers had been "No." Each of the panel members had advised against that approach, and Robert was worried.

Robert was right to be worried. There has been a great deal written about filters generally, much of it readily available at sites like www.ala.org, www.fepproject .org (Free Expression Policy Project, Brennan Center for Justice at NYU School of Law), www.kff.org (Kaiser Family Foundation), www.consumerreports.org, and others linked from the Office for Intellectual Freedom section of the ALA website. The most important point to remember is that *all filters underblock and overblock—they don't block sites they should, and they do block sites they shouldn't, most of them protected by the First Amendment, even for minors. All of them give parents and libraries a false sense of security, and they cannot take the place of educating users, particularly children, to use the Internet safely.* This excerpt from the ALA's "Libraries and the Internet Toolkit" expresses it well:

> Filters do not protect children, education does. As the National Research Council pointed out in its 2002 report, Youth, Pornography, and the Internet, "Swimming pools can be dangerous for children. To protect them, one can install locks, put up fences, and deploy pool alarms. All these measures are helpful, but by far the most important thing that one can do for one's children is to teach them to swim." Similarly, the more children and parents know about the Internet and Internet safety, the better equipped they will be to protect themselves and enjoy their time online.[5]

Libraries have approached the question of whether or how to use filters from a variety of perspectives. Under the Children's Internet Protection Act (CIPA), school and public libraries that want to receive certain federal funds from the E-Rate program must use some form of "technology protection measures"

Federal Laws Regulating Internet Access

Children's Internet Protection Act (CIPA)
47 U.S.C. § 254(h)(5) and 20 U.S.C. § 9134(f)

The Children's Internet Protection Act requires public schools and libraries that receive federal E-Rate discounts or Library Services and Technology Act (LSTA) grant payments for Internet access to certify that they have adopted an Internet use policy that requires the use of a "technology protection measure," that is, blocking or filtering technology.

The filtering technology must be installed on all computers in the school, including computers used by faculty and staff. It must be configured to block minors' access to visual depictions that are obscene, child pornography, or harmful to minors; and block adults' access to visual depictions that are obscene or child pornography.

CIPA permits an administrator to disable the technology during use by an adult in order to permit access for "bona fide research or other lawful purposes." The law does not forbid unblocking a wrongfully blocked website that does not contain materials that fall under the law's visual depictions that are obscene, child pornography, or harmful to minors.

CIPA imposes no requirements on schools and libraries that do not receive federal E-Rate discounts or LSTA grants.

Neighborhood Children's Internet Protection Act (NCIPA)
47 U.S.C. § 254(l)

The Neighborhood Children's Internet Protection Act requires public schools and libraries receiving federal E-Rate discounts to draft and implement an Internet safety policy. The policy must address the following issues:

1. access by minors to inappropriate matter on the Internet and World Wide Web;
2. the safety and security of minors when using electronic mail, chat rooms, and other forms of direct electronic communications;
3. unauthorized access, including so-called "hacking," and other unlawful activities by minors online;
4. unauthorized disclosure, use, and dissemination of personal identification information regarding minors; and
5. measures designed to restrict minors' access to materials harmful to minors.

Before adopting the Internet safety policy, the school or library must hold at least one public hearing or meeting to allow the community to address the proposed policy.

NCIPA states that the determination of what material is "inappropriate" is left to the local school board, educational agency, or library; no federal agency may interfere in that determination. The determination of what policy to adopt is left solely to the discretion of the local body.

Other Laws Regulating Internet Access

At the present time, twenty-three states have Internet filtering laws that apply to public schools or libraries. Most of these laws only require that schools or libraries adopt Internet use policies that address minors' access to online materials that are obscene, "harmful to minors," or are child pornography. A small number of states require public schools or libraries to install filtering software on computers. The National Conference of State Legislatures (link below) maintains a frequently updated website with information about state laws regulating Internet use or access.

Additional Resources

Bocher, Robert. "FAQ on E-Rate Compliance with the Children's Internet Protection Act" (http://dpi.wi.gov/pld/pdf/cipafaq.pdf).

Federal Communications Commission. "In the Matter of Federal-State Joint Board on Universal Service Children's Internet Protection Act, CC Docket No. 96-45" (July 24, 2003) (http://hraunfoss.fcc.gov/edocs_public/attachmatch/FCC-03–188A1.pdf).

Federal Communications Commission, Report and Order 11-125, Report and Regulations Implementing CIPA (August 21, 2011) (http://transition.fcc.gov/Daily_Releases/Daily_Business/2011/db0819/FCC-11-125A1.pdf).

Institute of Museum and Library Services. "The Children's Internet Protection Act" (http://www.imls.gov/about/cipa.shtm).

National Conference of State Legislatures. "State Internet Filtering Laws" (http://www.ncsl.org/programs/lis/CIP/filterlaws.htm).

(software filters) and adopt an Internet safety policy (usually the IUP). Some libraries, usually after a public discussion, decided not to use filters at all and turned down the funds. Some libraries decided the money wasn't worth the cost to comply and turned down the funds. Some libraries were required to use filters, whether or not they received the funds, because of local or state ordinances. Some libraries decided to install several different filters and let the users decide which one to use, or, for adults, none at all. Some libraries decided to install filters and enable the fewest categories possible. Some libraries decided to install filters and enable all categories, which was probably how the software arrived from the producer "out of the box." Since filters were originally developed to help businesses keep their employees from frittering away company time, the categories may include some not appropriate for public libraries, like "sports," "shopping," "humor," or even "other."

ALA and the ACLU filed lawsuits to have CIPA declared unconstitutional, because they believed the law infringed on the First Amendment right of library users to receive constitutionally protected speech. The various suits were combined into one to bring before the U.S. Supreme Court, resulting in *United States, et al. v. American Library Association, et al.*

In a plurality decision, the Court held that CIPA complied with constitutional demands, and public libraries began installing filters if they wanted to receive E-Rate discounts. In his concurring opinion, Justice Kennedy noted that

> *libraries that did not unblock specific websites or did not disable the filter without significant delay risked a legal challenge, stating "if it is shown that an adult user's election to view constitutionally protected Internet material is burdened in some other substantial way, that would be the subject for an as-applied challenge."* Kennedy, J., concurring, *United States v. Am. Library Ass'n*, 539 U.S. 194, 215 (2003) (emphasis added)

The suits that the ALA and ACLU filed claimed that CIPA was unconstitutional on a "facial" basis, which means that the law can never be enforced in a way—on its face—that does not violate constitutional rights. Justice Kennedy was warning libraries that they need to develop a way to provide unfiltered Internet access for adults, upon their demand. If a library cannot disable the filters quickly, particularly for an adult, it may find itself faced with an "as applied" lawsuit. In this case, the law itself remains in force, but the way the library provides access—as it applies the law—violates the user's First Amendment right to receive material. A library that ignores this advice from the U.S. Supreme Court may be inviting trouble, and a case now pending in Washington involving this issue may answer some of these questions.

United States v. American Library Association

The American Library Association joined with local public libraries and library users to challenge the constitutionality of the Children's Internet Protection Act (CIPA). On June 23, 2003, the Supreme Court upheld the Children's Internet Protection Act, but without enough justices for a majority opinion (called a plurality decision).

Four justices, led by Chief Justice Rehnquist, rejected the idea that the public forum analysis applied to the library's provision of Internet access, ruling that CIPA's filtering requirement was a constitutional condition imposed on institutions in exchange for government funding. The four justices said that any problems with filters blocking constitutionally protected websites were cured by the provisions in CIPA which allowed adults to ask the library to disable the Internet filter.

Justice Rehnquist's reliance on the disabling provisions as a cure for any unconstitutionality was based on the U.S. solicitor general's position that librarians could unblock filters for adults without any explanation or need to ascertain that the request was bona fide. According to the Court, "adults need only to ask for the filter to be disabled. There is no need for the user to provide an explanation for his or her request."

Based upon the plurality's endorsement of the solicitor general's position that libraries would disable filters for adults without delay, both Justice Kennedy and Justice Breyer concurred with the plurality's decision. Justice Kennedy warned, however, that if the rights of adults to view material on the Internet was burdened in any way, it could give rise to a claim in the future that CIPA was unconstitutional as applied to those users:

> If some libraries do not have the capacity to unblock specific Web sites or to disable the filter or if it is shown that an adult user's election to view constitutionally protected Internet material is burdened in some other substantial way, that would be the subject for an as-applied challenge.

The multiple opinions issued by the Supreme Court in *United States v. American Library Association* make plain that disabling Internet filters for adults is critical to the constitutional use of filters in the public libraries.

Without the guarantee that adult library users could disable the filter or unblock a filtered website, there were insufficient votes on the Court for the majority necessary to uphold the statute.

Currently, a group of library users in Washington State are suing a library for failing to disable its Internet filter at the request of adults. That lawsuit, *Bradburn v. North Central Regional Library District,* is pending before the federal courts in Washington State, awaiting a decision on whether the library's policy of not disabling the filter or unblocking websites for adult users violates the First Amendment.

Additional Resources

United States v. American Library Association, 539 U.S. 194 (2003)
Sarah Bradburn v. North Central Regional Library District, CV-06–0327-EFS, E.D. Washington

CASE STUDY 3

Emily was at the public desk when Eileen, a regular at the public Internet stations, came up and complained that the fellow at the other station was looking at something "really awful." Emily's board had decided not to install software filters, mainly because they were too expensive compared to the amount of E-Rate money the library might receive. They settled, instead, on the "tap on the shoulder" approach when someone complained, and this incident was the first complaint she'd received. Emily was nervous as she approached the man. She "tapped him on the shoulder" and explained that someone had complained and he'd have to look at sites more appropriate for a library. He replied that it's a free country and that he could look at anything "he damn well wanted to."

The "tap on the shoulder" is an approach some libraries have adopted to control "inappropriate" sites if users display them on Internet monitors. While for some, the "tap" is a figure of speech, for others, they are expected to touch the person, an action often discouraged by governing bodies because of liability issues.

As you might imagine, this approach is riddled with subjective judgment and vague standards. Determining what content will invoke the "tap" is a major problem with this method, because the library staff does not have the authority to decide if a particular site is obscene and not constitutionally protected, or merely pornographic and protected. Any attempt to block a user's access based on an assessment of the content may violate the user's corollary First Amendment right to receive "speech," or information.

There's also the issue of the consequences:

- Is the user kicked off the Internet?
- Kicked out of the library?
- For how long?
- Who decides? and
- Can the user appeal the decision?

If the library relies on the "tap" without a policy, it does not have the written authority to enforce the procedure, and it may be accused of violating the user's Fifth Amendment right to due process. In other words, it's just not fair to boot a user off the terminal or even out of the library, if he can't figure out, in advance, what content will result in a penalty. The problem may escalate if the staff member calls in private security or the police if the user refuses, as in this case, to refrain from viewing the "offensive" sites. Unless the user is violating some other library regulation not related to content, the library may find itself in a very sticky liability situation.

Further, if the library writes a policy that attempts to describe the offensive content, it may be in trouble for trying to enforce a policy which is facially unconstitutional, that is, it cannot be enforced without violating the user's constitutional rights.

CASE STUDY 4

Richard was disappointed and angry. He couldn't go home on the bus like he usually did, because both of his parents were busy that afternoon and didn't want him to be home alone. The only place they let him go was the public library. He thought it might be okay if he could get on the Internet and get into a chat room for the new Prince of Persia, his current favorite. When his turn at the Internet finally came, he couldn't get anywhere—the library wouldn't let him get into any chat rooms or any of his online games. The library only allowed important uses of the computer, so no gaming, chat rooms, or Facebook allowed. Stupid, Stupid, Stupid!

I think Richard has good reason to be angry. Some libraries decided not to allow any Internet use that wasn't educational or serious, at least for children. Although they wouldn't allow any gaming at their Internet stations, they had books and periodicals about games in the collection. By now, most libraries have reversed that position, and many are actively promoting gaming as a way to bring in a previously disinterested segment of their communities. They are also using games as a way to develop digital literacy, particularly for those users with no other access to the Internet and computers.

Libraries were also concerned that allowing access to chat rooms and social networking sites might open a door for "perverts." While protecting children from predators is a serious consideration, the best way to keep children away from predators is to teach them—and their parents—how to use the Internet safely, not simply to block use of those sites. More and more, schools are requiring students to work on group or team projects that rely on chat rooms or networking sites like Facebook. Without access, they may not be able to do their homework, and, again, that access is most critical for students who have to rely on the library for Internet access. Even the FCC recognized the importance of allowing access to social media on school and library computers in August 2011, when it reversed the requirement to block those websites for minors.

Charlie, known by his friends as a "curmudgeonly old coot," walked into the library to look up a tool manufacturer's address that he had left at home. He hadn't been in the library in years, but he knew they had Internet stations for the public, and he figured it would just take a minute to look up the address there. Without it, his trip into town to go to the post office was a waste of time and gas. He managed to find an empty workstation, but when he tried to use it, the computer wouldn't let him in without entering his library card number. He hadn't had a card for years—never used the library, after all—and after the librarian told him he couldn't use the Internet without one, he got so angry that he refused to get one then. He wasn't shy about letting everyone know.

The library certainly didn't make a friend here. Some libraries have set up systems to require a library card for use, often seen as an extension of their policies that deny circulation privileges to users outside their city or county area. While that practice may free up computer time for their taxpayers, not everyone who pays taxes has a library card. There's also a question about how denying access to this library service might infringe on a corollary First Amendment right to use a public library (see the discussion of the *Kreimer v. Bureau of Police for the Town of Morristown* case in chapters 4 and 7). An easy solution is to provide a card that will provide a number for the computer but won't allow the user to check out any library material.

QUESTIONS TO ASK

- Does the library have a procedure for handling complaints about the Internet?
- Does the library have a policy that details expected behavior when using the Internet?
- Is the policy readily available to users?
- Does the entire staff understand the policy?
- If your library uses software filters:

    Are there prominent notifications that filters are in use?

    Are all categories enabled or just a few?

    Is there a procedure to disable the filter or unblock a site for an adult? If so, who decides, and how long does it take?

NOTES

1. June Pinnell-Stephens, "Lester Asheim in Cyberspace: A Tribute to Sound Reasoning," *American Libraries* 33, no. 9 (October 2002): 70+.
2. Although this paper was written (but never published) in 1997, the section used here is still current and has remained the same with the exception of the ALA interpretation.
3. "I shall not today attempt further to define the kinds of material I understand to be embraced within that shorthand description ["hard-core pornography"]; and perhaps I could never succeed in intelligibly doing so. But I know it when I see it, and the motion picture involved in this case is not that." Justice Potter Stewart, concurring opinion in *Jacobellis v. Ohio*, 378 U.S. 184 (1964).
4. June Pinnell-Stephens, "Libraries: A Misunderstood American Value," *American Libraries* 30, no. 6 (June/July 1999): 76–78+.
5. American Library Association, www.ala.org/ala/aboutala/offices/oif/iftoolkits/litoolkit/librarieschildren.cfm (accessed September 8, 2009).

CHAPTER 4

Not the Collection: Meeting Rooms, Exhibits, and Programs

Ironically, one of the easiest ways for a library to get into trouble doesn't include the collection at all. Libraries that offer exhibit spaces or meeting rooms have been the focus of lawsuits because they violated the users' rights to free expression (First Amendment), due process (Fifth Amendment), and/or equal protection (Fourteenth Amendment). Several of these cases have occurred fairly recently, and some of them are currently under litigation, so it's important to keep track of new developments.

Providing these spaces gives the library an opportunity to place itself at the heart of its community. With so few shared public spaces available in most cities and towns, the library can offer these resources for users to share local information and to meet for various civic, educational, and recreational occasions. The need for a place to gather—to be a community—is too great for the library to risk alienating its users by making unnecessary blunders in policy.

PUBLIC FORUM

At issue in this discussion is how the library defines its spaces under the public forum doctrine, and that definition depends on what level of activity and access is allowed—that is, who decides the content that goes into it—in a specific area. An *open* or *traditional* public forum is the soapbox in the town square—for libraries, it might be the equivalent of its parking lot or sidewalks. A *designated* or *limited* public form is limited to a particular type of activity under a particular set of circumstances—for libraries, a meeting room or exhibit space. A *closed* or *nonpublic* forum is one not open for general access—in libraries it might be the main collection area or a bulletin board restricted to library or other government information.

When my library commission was struggling with an appropriate exhibits policy after a complaint, this table helped them understand the types and limitations of the different public forums:

TYPE	ELIGIBLE GROUPS	CONTENT
Open or traditional public forum	All	No restriction possible
Designated or limited public forum	All groups that meet a content- and viewpoint-neutral definition	No content or viewpoint restriction is possible
Closed or non-public forum	Library or related governmental units	Determined by the library

In the open category, the activity most often occurs in areas more likely to be controlled by the police and is not often a problem for the library. Areas designated as closed forums aren't a problem, because the library controls all use and content. Most of the problems seem to arise in the areas that fall under the designated category, typically the meeting rooms and exhibit spaces. In these cases, the library gets to decide which groups use the facility, and it often tries to control the content, as well. That's when it gets into trouble.

Public Forum Doctrine and the Library

A *public forum* is a public space or a government-owned property in which the public can exercise the First Amendment right to speak or receive ideas. *Public forum doctrine* is the set of rules developed by the courts to identify a public forum and to define the scope of First Amendment protections extended to those using a public forum for free speech activities.

The Supreme Court has identified two kinds of public forums open for free exercise of speech activities. The first is the *traditional public forum,* places "held in trust for the use of the public and, time out of mind, . . . used for purposes of assembly, communicating thoughts between citizens, and discussing public questions," such as parks, sidewalks, and public squares. The second type of public forum is the *designated public forum,* space or property that the government has intentionally opened for expressive activity by part or all of the public.

When the government opens a designated public forum, it can choose to open the forum to all speakers for all kinds of expression, like a traditional public forum, or it can choose to restrict the forum by reserving it for particular speakers or expressive activities. A forum that is designated for the use of certain speakers or for the exercise of certain kinds of speech activities is often called a *limited public forum.*

In a public forum, the government may not restrict speech based solely on its content unless it meets a very high legal standard, called *strict scrutiny.* In order to meet this standard, the government must show that its rule is necessary to achieve a compelling government interest; that the rule is narrowly drawn to achieve that interest; and that there are no less-restrictive alternatives available that will accomplish the government's goal. Government restrictions on speech seldom meet this standard.

The government can, however, make content-neutral rules that regulate the time, place, and manner of speech in a public forum. Such rules must be narrowly drawn to serve an important government interest and must operate without regard for the identity of the individual, the content of the individual's speech, or the viewpoint expressed by the individual.

In its opinion in *Kreimer v. Bureau of Police for the Town of Morristown,* the Third Circuit Court of Appeals ruled unequivocally that *the public library is a designated public forum.* Applying public forum doctrine to determine whether the library administration could limit access to the library, the court held that the Morristown Public Library created a designated public forum when it intentionally opened the library to the public for the specified purposes of reading, studying, and using the library's materials. Because the library had not opened its doors for other speech activities, such as public speechmaking or passing out pamphlets, the court further held that the library was a *limited public forum,* open only for those expressive activities consistent with the nature of the library and the right to access information.

In accord with earlier decisions concerning access to a public forum, the *Kreimer* court ruled the library, as a limited public forum, could not exclude persons or groups from its facilities solely because of a disagreement with their views, or to avoid controversy or public disapproval. The library could, however, establish reasonable rules to regulate non-expressive activities, if those rules were applied without discrimination to all library users and if the rules were intended to promote safety or efficient access to the library's materials or services.

Additional Resources

Kreimer v. Bureau of Police for the Town of Morristown, 958 F.2d 1242, 1256 (3d Cir. 1992)

The local PFLAG (Parents, Friends and Family of Lesbians and Gays) group had signed up for the main exhibit space in the downtown library almost a year ago. They wanted to highlight the gay and lesbian community just before the city's Rainbow March, and they had received the library's approval for the display they had outlined in the application. Just after Susan and Emily, part of the PFLAG group, finished putting the display in place and left, Stephen, the library director, walked by and saw it. He immediately removed some of the objects in the display and went to his office to call the mayor. Stephen, having received the mayor's blessing, then removed the rest of the display. When Susan and Emily came to add a couple of items to the display the next day, they were outraged. They had been careful to follow all of the library's policies and procedures, and now their display had been censored.

Stephen and the mayor may be looking at a lawsuit. PFLAG qualified to use the exhibit area as a local, nonprofit group engaged in "cultural, educational, recreational, or informational activities," the definition in the library's policy. They also followed the proper procedures by submitting a description and diagram of the display they wanted to post, which the library approved in writing. When Stephen took the display down, he violated the library's policy and the First Amendment right to free speech of the PFLAG members, despite receiving the mayor's permission.

Once the library created a designated public forum, as it did in this case by allowing local nonprofit groups that met the established criteria to use the exhibit space, it was obligated to let *every group that meets the criteria* use the space and to apply the same procedures and regulations to each group. Further, the library was prohibited from limiting the displays themselves based on the content or viewpoint of the material. Any limitation has to be based on the time, place, or manner of use, not the content. The only exception might be to material that presents a public hazard, like explosives or perishable food.

In all complaints about the use of meeting rooms or exhibits, the policy needs to remind users that the library does not endorse the views of those who have organized a meeting or produced a display—the library makes the space available to all groups that meet the written criteria, and it makes the resource available to all users.

The library's policy must:

Describe each area, e.g.,

- meeting rooms
- display cases
- children's room
- lobby
- main part of the library

Determine the type of forum of each area, e.g.,

- the exhibit case is a designated public forum
- the main part of the library is a closed public forum

Define eligibility for use of each area, e.g.,

- nonprofit organizations in the county engaged in cultural, educational, recreational, intellectual, or charitable activities
- library only

Establish regulations for use of each area, e.g.,

- each display may be scheduled for a one-month period
- no drinks allowed in the children's room

Provide a means of appeal, e.g.,

- reconsideration handled in the same manner as other complaints about library resources
- because of limited time in the case of displays, an expedited process may be necessary

Court Opinion

IN THE UNITED STATES DISTRICT COURT
FOR THE DISTRICT OF ALASKA Case No. AOI-0173 CV (JKS)
PFLAG/ANCHORAGE ALASKA CHAPTER OF PARENTS, FAMILIES AND
FRIENDS OF LESBIANS AND GAYS, et al., Plaintiffs
vs.
MUNICIPALITY OF ANCHORAGE, Defendant.

On June 27, 2001, pursuant to Rule 65(b) of the Federal Rules of Civil Procedure, Plaintiffs moved for a preliminary injunction against the Municipality of Anchorage barring impermissible content discrimination in the displays at municipal libraries, and for immediate reinstatement of their "Celebrating Diversity Under the Midnight Sun" exhibit for not less than 30 days. The exhibit was originally placed according to the terms of an understanding between Plaintiff Janet Richardson and authorized agents of the Municipality of Anchorage permitted in conformity with the then-existing regulations and policies governing exhibits and displays by community organizations at the municipal libraries.

The Court took limited testimony on Friday, June 29, 2001, and heard final argument on Tuesday, July 3, 2001. This Order will constitute the Court's finding of fact and conclusions of law. To the extent that a finding of fact has been mislabeled a conclusion of law and vice-versa, the careful reader should be charitable. Judicial decisions, like exhibits evaluated under the First Amendment, should be considered as a whole.

Findings of Fact

On June 4, 2001, Plaintiffs set up an exhibit titled "Celebrating Diversity Under the Midnight Sun" at Loussac Library. The exhibit had been provisionally permitted by authorized agents of the Municipality charged with supervising displays and exhibits by community organizations at municipal libraries. Viewed as a whole, the exhibit was consistent with exhibits previously approved for display by the Municipality.

The evidence shows that the Municipality created a designated public forum at the Loussac Library, limited to posters, pictures and the like, for posting on the walls, and that this public forum was widely used by a variety of community groups. The Municipality has not fashioned a policy that meaningfully distinguished between "promotional" as distinct from "educational" exhibits by community organizations for presentation at the Loussac Library. The Municipality did not rely upon a clear and unambiguous policy in this case when it elected to remove Plaintiffs' exhibit.

Furthermore, the Municipality's objection to the promotional nature of Plaintiffs' exhibit was clearly an afterthought. The original objection to the exhibit was that it involved the Library's elevators. That objection raised three concerns: (a) safety; (b) interactivity, which Municipal witnesses explained as forcing an unwilling captive audience to become personally involved in the exhibit; and (c) that the exhibit encouraged horseplay by children not properly supervised by parents or guardians. While these concerns may have justified the Municipality in excluding the elevators from the exhibit as a reasonable time, place and manner regulation, none of these concerns addressed the exhibit as a whole, nor justified removing the parts of the exhibit adjacent to the elevators. Plaintiffs themselves offered to move the exhibit away from the elevators.

Conclusions of Law

This Court has jurisdiction over the subject matter and the parties to the action. See 28 U.S.C. §§ 1331, 1343; 42 U.S.C. § 1983.

While Plaintiffs rely on both the United States Constitution and the Constitution of the State of Alaska, only Federal law is considered in this Order. The Ninth Circuit has adopted a "sliding scale" approach to the issuance of injunctive relief, under which the Court is to balance the harm threatened to the parties and the likelihood of Plaintiffs' success on the merits.

Plaintiffs face the threat of irreparable injury to their First Amendment rights if an injunction is not issued, and they have no adequate remedy at law.

The Municipality will be adequately protected if an injunction is issued.

The balance of hardships therefore weighs heavily in favor of Plaintiffs.

Plaintiffs have shown a likelihood of success on the merits of their constitutional claims.

The Municipality's concerns about the elevators can be addressed by eliminating them from the exhibit. The distinction the Municipality currently makes between exhibits that are educational and those that are promotional relies on the ambiguities and vagueness of those terms. It does not appear that the Municipality has applied these terms consistently. See *Hopper v. City of Pasco,* 241 F.3d 1067 (9th Cir. 2001).

it is Therefore Ordered:

The Municipality of Anchorage, and its agents, employees, or representatives, are hereby prohibited from engaging in impermissible viewpoint discrimination in the displays at municipal libraries. The Municipality must immediately, and in no case later than Thursday, July 12, 2001, allow for the reinstallation of the "Celebrating Diversity Under the Midnight Sun" exhibit. The exhibit shall be displayed in a form as close as possible to the original design, but without involving the elevators, and shall be placed in the general area adjacent to the elevators where the exhibit was originally installed for not less than 30 days, according to the terms of the understanding between Plaintiff Richardson and the Municipality. The Municipality shall be responsible for the reinstallation work; Plaintiffs are encouraged to supervise and/ or participate in the set-up to ensure that the work is done to their satisfaction. This preliminary injunction shall extend from the date of this Order until October 15, 2001, or until a trial can be held on this matter. Plaintiffs may recover their costs and a reasonable attorney fee upon proper motion brought pursuant to 42 U.S.C. § 1988. This Order and the accompanying judgment granting a preliminary injunction are immediately appealable. See 28 U.S.C. § 1292(a)(1); *Self-Realization Fellowship Church v. Ananda Church of Self-Realization,* 59 F.3d 902 (9th Cir. 1995).

—JAMES K. SINGLET, JR., United States District Judge

Exhibits/Meeting Room Complaints
Sample Language from the Fairbanks (Alaska) North Star Borough Public Library

Reconsideration and Appeal—Patrons concerned about material in, or scheduled for, display spaces are welcome to discuss those concerns with a professional staff member and/or the Library Director. Patrons who want the Library Selection Committee to reconsider material in a display space will be given Request for Reconsideration forms and informed of the reconsideration procedure.

Since displays are exhibited for a relatively short time and early notification of planned displays will be provided through advance notice and other means, patrons are requested to return the completed Request for Reconsideration form as soon as possible after a display opens.

The Library Selection Committee will meet and make a decision within two Fairbanks North Star Borough office working days of receipt of the Request for Reconsideration form following the opening of a display.

The Library Director will use appropriate expedited means to communicate the Selection Committee's decision to the patron(s) who submitted the Request for Reconsideration.

The Library Commission shall hear appeals from the Library Selection Committee's decisions for reconsideration of materials in a display space. To the extent practicable, the Commission shall hear the appeal within five Fairbanks North Star Borough working days of the Library Director's receipt of an appeal from a patron. Public notice of the appeal hearing on a display shall be given no less than 48 hours prior to the hearing.

The Commission may choose to have a hearing officer. The hearing officer will advise the Commission on administrative hearing procedures and may be present at the appeal hearing.

Written comments will be accepted up to the time of the hearing. Public comments will be taken at the hearing and will be limited to no more than three minutes per person. Each person may speak only once; however, the hearing officer or members of the Commission may question a member of the public to obtain further relevant information. The Commission may arrange for additional testimony from expert witnesses.

The decision of the Commission shall be the final administrative remedy in this appeal process. The Commission's decision may be appealed to a court of competent jurisdiction.

The display being challenged will remain in place during the reconsideration process.

Exhibit Spaces and Bulletin Boards
An Interpretation of the Library Bill of Rights

Libraries often provide exhibit spaces and bulletin boards. The uses made of these spaces should conform to the Library Bill of Rights: Article I states, "Materials should not be excluded because of the origin, background, or views of those contributing to their creation." Article II states, "Materials should not be proscribed or removed because of partisan or doctrinal disapproval." Article VI maintains that exhibit space should be made available "on an equitable basis, regardless of the beliefs or affiliations of individuals or groups requesting their use."

In developing library exhibits, staff members should endeavor to present a broad spectrum of opinion and a variety of viewpoints. Libraries should not shrink from developing exhibits because of controversial content or because of the beliefs or affiliations of those whose work is represented. Just as libraries do not endorse the viewpoints of those whose work is represented in their collections, libraries also do not endorse the beliefs or viewpoints of topics that may be the subject of library exhibits.

Exhibit areas often are made available for use by community groups. Libraries should formulate a written policy for the use of these exhibit areas to assure that space is provided on an equitable basis to all groups that request it.

Written policies for exhibit space use should be stated in inclusive rather than exclusive terms. For example, a policy that the library's exhibit space is open "to organizations engaged in educational, cultural, intellectual, or charitable activities" is an inclusive statement of the limited uses of the exhibit space. This defined limitation would permit religious groups to use the exhibit space because they engage in intellectual activities, but would exclude most commercial uses of the exhibit space.

A publicly supported library may designate use of exhibit space for strictly library-related activities, provided that this limitation is viewpoint neutral and clearly defined.

Libraries may include in this policy rules regarding the time, place, and manner of use of the exhibit space, so long as the rules are content neutral and are applied in the same manner to all groups wishing to use the space. A library may wish to limit access to exhibit space to groups within the community served by the library. This practice is acceptable provided that the same rules and regulations apply to everyone, and that exclusion is not made on the basis of the doctrinal, religious, or political beliefs of the potential users.

The library should not censor or remove an exhibit because some members of the community may disagree with its content. Those who object to the content of any exhibit held at the library should be able to submit their complaint and/or their own exhibit proposal to be judged according to the policies established by the library.

Libraries may wish to post a permanent notice near the exhibit area stating that the library does not advocate or endorse the viewpoints of exhibits or exhibitors.

Libraries that make bulletin boards available to public groups for posting notices of public interest should develop criteria for the use of these spaces based on the same considerations as those outlined above. Libraries may wish to develop criteria regarding the size of material to be displayed, the length of time materials may remain on the bulletin board, the frequency with which material may be posted for the same group, and the geographic area from which notices will be accepted.

Adopted July 2, 1991, by the ALA Council; amended June 30, 2004.

http://ifmanual.org/exhibitspaces

Marianne tried to reserve the library's small meeting room for a "Celebration of the Bible" for the ladies group at her church, but Dean, the director, said that "religious services" weren't allowed in the library. She tried to explain that the celebration wasn't a "service" but more like a study group, and the library allowed other study groups. When Dean said that the other groups weren't religious, Marianne almost lost her temper. Instead, she asked for a copy of the policy and whatever form she had to file to object to this denial. As soon as she left the library, she called Emily, a member of the ladies group, whose husband was a lawyer.

For many years, libraries usually excluded religious or political content from displays and users from their meeting rooms. Starting in the mid- to late 1990s, there have been a number of lawsuits addressing that practice, and most of them were successful. Your library should look at its policies to be sure it doesn't discriminate against those groups on the basis of the content of their speech, whether in a meeting room or display. As in the previous case, if the library makes its resources available to one group, it must make them available to all groups that meet the access criteria, regardless of their messages, because it has established a designated public forum.

Since meeting rooms are often in high demand, libraries need to establish content- and viewpoint-neutral procedures and regulations to control access fairly. Some libraries have said they don't want the library to turn into a church, but a regulation that prevents any user from reserving the library's meeting room more than once a month because of high demand prevents that problem and does so in a content-neutral manner. Other libraries have tried to restrict their meeting rooms on the basis of singing, which they claim makes the meeting a church service. If those libraries applied that restriction to their own children's programs, they couldn't use the rooms, either.

If your library has a number of meeting rooms or exhibit areas, it can establish each as a different type of forum with different regulations for access or use. This flexibility helps large libraries offer some of their rooms for public access and reserve some for library use only. It can also help small libraries set aside some of its space for preschool story time at a certain time on certain days and then open that space to general use at other times.

One potential problem with allowing political groups to reserve a display space may occur if the library is a polling place. State law often prohibits "electioneering" within a certain number of feet from the polling place, and any display that supports a particular candidate or ballot issue would have to be covered or removed on election day.

Meeting Rooms
An Interpretation of the Library Bill of Rights

Many libraries provide meeting rooms for individuals and groups as part of a program of service. Article VI of the Library Bill of Rights states that such facilities should be made available to the public served by the given library "on an equitable basis, regardless of the beliefs or affiliations of individuals or groups requesting their use."

Libraries maintaining meeting room facilities should develop and publish policy statements governing use. These statements can properly define time, place, or manner of use; such qualifications should not pertain to the content of a meeting or to the beliefs or affiliations of the sponsors. These statements should be made available in any commonly used language within the community served.

If meeting rooms in libraries supported by public funds are made available to the general public for non-library sponsored events, the library may not exclude any group based on the subject matter to be discussed or based on the ideas that the group advocates. For example, if a library allows charities and sports clubs to discuss their activities in library meeting rooms, then the library should not exclude partisan political or religious groups from discussing their activities in the same facilities. If a library opens its meeting rooms to a wide variety of civic organizations, then the library may not deny access to a religious organization. Libraries may wish to post a permanent notice near the meeting room stating that the library does not advocate or endorse the viewpoints of meetings or meeting room users.

Written policies for meeting room use should be stated in inclusive rather than exclusive terms. For example, a policy that the library's facilities are open "to organizations engaged in educational, cultural, intellectual, or charitable activities" is an inclusive statement of the limited uses to which the facilities may be put. This defined limitation would permit religious groups to use the facilities because they engage in intellectual activities, but would exclude most commercial uses of the facility.

A publicly supported library may limit use of its meeting rooms to strictly "library-related" activities, provided that the limitation is clearly circumscribed and is viewpoint neutral.

Written policies may include limitations on frequency of use, and whether or not meetings held in library meeting rooms must be open to the public. If state and local laws permit private as well as public sessions of meetings in libraries, libraries may choose to offer both options. The same standard should be applicable to all.

If meetings are open to the public, libraries should include in their meeting room policy statement a section that addresses admission fees. If admission fees are permitted, libraries shall seek to make it possible that these fees do not limit access to individuals who may be unable to pay, but who wish to attend the meeting. Article V of the Library Bill of Rights states that "a person's right to use a library should not be denied or abridged because of origin, age, background, or views." It is inconsistent with Article V to restrict indirectly access to library meeting rooms based on an individual's or group's ability to pay for that access.

Adopted July 2, 1991, by the ALA Council.

http://ifmanual.org/meetingrooms

Library Meeting Rooms and Religious Groups

A public library is not legally required to provide public access to its meeting rooms or other facilities. But when the public library chooses to open its meeting rooms, display cases, and literature tables to public use, those facilities become a designated public forum.

As such, the library cannot exclude speakers or groups from using the library's facilities because of the content of their speech or a disagreement with their views. Nor can the library exclude a group from its facilities to avoid controversy or public disapproval. Libraries that discriminate against a group or individual on these grounds risk legal liability for their actions.

A particular concern is the exclusion of groups on the basis of their religious character or their intent to engage in religious activity. A library whose meeting room policy excludes religious groups or activities from a library's meeting rooms can violate the Free Speech Clause of the First Amendment.

In one instance, the Concerned Women for America (CWA) sued a Texas public library when the library refused to allow a prayer group sponsored by the CWA to use its auditorium for a meeting. In its opinion, *Concerned Women for America, Inc. v. Lafayette County,* the Fifth Circuit Court of Appeals ruled in favor of the CWA, holding that the library could not exclude speakers from its meeting room based upon the content of their speech when it had opened its meeting rooms to the public. The court ruled that the library's meeting rooms were a designated public forum, and that the library could not exclude a speaker or a group from its meeting rooms unless the exclusion served a compelling state interest and there was no less restrictive means to achieve that goal. It further found that any potential disruption by the CWA could be addressed by imposing reasonable time, place, or manner restrictions on access to the auditorium that were applicable to all users and were imposed without reference to the content of the users' speech.

More recently, an Ohio public library refused to allow the Citizens for Community Values (CCV) to hold a "Politics and the Pulpit" event in its meeting room, because the library believed that the event would include prayer and praise, which a library administrator believed to be "inherent elements of a religious worship service." The group sued the library.

The court reviewed the library's policy and practices and found that the library opened its meeting rooms to a wide range of groups for a wide range of expressive activities, including meetings, discussions, lectures, and other nonprofit activities that serve the community, creating a limited public forum. It also found that the CCV's proposed presentation was compatible with the allowed uses of the meeting rooms. In its opinion, *Citizens for Community Values, Inc. v. Upper Arlington Public Library,* it permanently enjoined the library from "severing out and excluding activities from its meeting rooms that it concludes are 'inherent elements of a religious service' or elements that are 'quintessentially religious.'"

The court also rejected the library's argument that its actions were justified by its compelling interest in not violating the Establishment Clause of the First Amendment.

The court held that providing meeting space to the CCV did not advance religion, as long as the library did not endorse the event and there was no evidence that religious groups would dominate the use of the library's meeting room.

In 2006, the Ninth Circuit Court of Appeals upheld a public library's policy excluding religious activity, on the grounds that the library had a legitimate interest in screening and excluding meeting room activities that could interfere with the library's primary mission. Because the group applying to use the meeting room advertised its event as a religious service, the library could exclude the event as inconsistent with the library's mission.

But the Ninth Circuit warned the library that the library had to exercise caution when trying to distinguish between ordinary religious activities and a worship service, and reminded the library that it could not prohibit religious groups from engaging in other religious activities in its meeting rooms, including reading the Bible, Bible discussions, Bible instruction, praying, singing, sharing testimony, and discussing political or social issues.

The Ninth Circuit's decision, *Faith Center Church Evangelistic Ministries, et al. v. Glover,* proved to have limited application. On further review, the federal district court administering the lawsuit on remand determined that the library's policy required librarians to inquire into and apply religious doctrine to determine whether a proposed activity constituted worship. This impermissibly entangled the library with the practice of religion in a manner forbidden by the Constitution. The court enjoined the library from enforcing the policy, on the grounds that it could not be applied without violating the First Amendment.

These three court decisions should discourage any library from drafting meeting room policies that exclude "religious worship." Such policies expose the library to possible lawsuits, especially if the library tries to determine when a group has crossed the line from a "meeting" to a "worship service." Meeting room policies can regulate the time, place, or manner of use as long as the regulations do not pertain to the content of a meeting or to the beliefs or affiliations of the sponsors.

Additional Resources

Concerned Women for America, Inc. v. Lafayette County, 883 F.2d 32, 34 (5th Cir. 1989)

Faith Center Church Evangelistic Ministries, et al. v. Glover, et al., 462 F.3d 1194 (9th Cir. 2006)

Citizens for Community Values, Inc. v. Upper Arlington Public Library, 2008 W.L. 3843579, 2008 U.S. Dist. LEXIS 85439 (S.D. Ohio 2008)

It had been busy at the reference desk that afternoon, but as Alice finally had a chance to catch her breath and look around, she noticed that someone seemed to be approaching other users and passing out pamphlets. The library had recently discovered that someone had been putting pamphlets inside books on the shelves, a practice against the library's policies, and Alice decided to see if this fellow was the culprit.

The distribution of literature is an area that libraries have tended to ignore in terms of a policy, but it's one that can cause problems. In this case, the library needs to define areas where distribution, whether in person or in a pamphlet holder, is controlled by the regulations for each designated forum. The regulations can be as simple or as complex as the staff will allow and range from "you can leave the flyers on the chairs in the lobby" to "you need to submit a sample to the director for approval and then, if approved, supply at least 100 copies no larger than 8.5 × 11 and check the pamphlet at least once a week." As before, it may be best to establish a number of different areas for different activities.

Another "not the collection" problem that libraries may encounter involves programs that the library itself sponsors. While this usually doesn't depend on the definition of the forum, it can be a problem if the library attempts to circumvent the requirement of equal access for groups the library may find "controversial." For example, if the library claims that a particular display case is a closed forum, for the library only, and then invites groups that it finds "acceptable" to supply displays, it may face a challenge from a group that was denied access to the cases.

Libraries may also receive complaints about the content of their programs, just as they do about the collection. Policies that protect the programs should remind users that the library provides material that serves the needs of all members of the community and must reflect a wide range of interests and values.

QUESTIONS TO ASK

- Does the library have meeting rooms or display cases? If so:

  Is there a policy that describes how each space may be used?

  Are there disclaimers in the display or program that state the library does not sponsor the material or its point of view?

  Does the staff understand the policy and implement it?

- Does the library set up its own displays or produce its own programs?

Distribution of Nonlibrary Literature

As part of its public service and information mission, the Fairbanks North Star Borough Public Library has established separate types of areas for the distribution of literature that is not part of the library's collection. Each area represents a different type of public forum and is controlled by different regulations.

The provision of these areas does not constitute library endorsement of the beliefs or viewpoints advocated by the literature or of the organizations responsible for it.

1. Library Lobby and William Berry Room (designated or limited public forum)

The library will make space available for literature, either as handouts or posted notices, from Fairbanks North Star Borough nonprofit organizations or governmental agencies engaged in educational, cultural, intellectual, or charitable activities.

A. General literature and literature primarily of interest to adults may be available in the lobby in areas designated by the Library Director on a space-available basis. Literature announcing non-recurring future events will have priority use of this space.

B. Literature of interest to children and their parents and teachers, as determined by library staff, may be available in the William Berry Room in areas designated by the Library Director on a space-available basis. Literature announcing non-recurring future events will have priority use of this space.

No solicitation or active distribution of literature will be permitted in either area.

2. Main Library (closed forum)

The library may make copies of documents addressing issues of local concern from governmental agencies or from private companies in fulfillment of governmental regulation available for public review. These documents will be available for an appropriate period of time and in an area designated by the Library Director, and they will not be available for circulation.

The library may distribute library-related material or other governmental resources at the discretion of the Library Director. No other distribution or display of literature and no solicitation will be permitted.

3. Library Entrance and Walkway (no public forum)

Because any restriction along the front walkway to the main entrance would hinder access by library users and present a potential safety hazard, there will be no distribution of literature or solicitation permitted in this area.

Library-Initiated Programs as a Resource
An Interpretation of the Library Bill of Rights

Library-initiated programs support the mission of the library by providing users with additional opportunities for information, education, and recreation. Article I of the Library Bill of Rights states: "Books and other library resources should be provided for the interest, information, and enlightenment of all people of the community the library serves."

Library-initiated programs take advantage of library staff expertise, collections, services and facilities to increase access to information and information resources. Library-initiated programs introduce users and potential users to the resources of the library and to the library's primary function as a facilitator of information access. The library may participate in cooperative or joint programs with other agencies, organizations, institutions, or individuals as part of its own effort to address information needs and to facilitate information access in the community the library serves.

Library-initiated programs on site and in other locations include, but are not limited to, speeches, community forums, discussion groups, demonstrations, displays, and live or media presentations.

Libraries serving multilingual or multicultural communities should make efforts to accommodate the information needs of those for whom English is a second language. Library-initiated programs that cross language and cultural barriers introduce otherwise underserved populations to the resources of the library and provide access to information.

Library-initiated programs "should not be proscribed or removed [or canceled] because of partisan or doctrinal disapproval" of the contents of the program or the views expressed by the participants, as stated in Article II of the Library Bill of Rights. Library sponsorship of a program does not constitute an endorsement of the content of the program or the views expressed by the participants, any more than the purchase of material for the library collection constitutes an endorsement of the contents of the material or the views of its creator.

Library-initiated programs are a library resource, and, as such, are developed in accordance with written guidelines, as approved and adopted by the library's policy-making body. These guidelines should include an endorsement of the Library Bill of Rights and set forth the library's commitment to free and open access to information and ideas for all users.

Library staff select topics, speakers and resource materials for library-initiated programs based on the interests and information needs of the community. Topics, speakers and resource materials are not excluded from library-initiated programs because of possible controversy. Concerns, questions or complaints about library-initiated programs are handled according to the same written policy and procedures that govern reconsiderations of other library resources.

Library-initiated programs are offered free of charge and are open to all. Article V of the Library Bill of Rights states: "A person's right to use a library should not be denied or abridged because of origin, age, background, or views."

The "right to use a library" encompasses all the resources the library offers, including the right to attend library-initiated programs. Libraries do not deny or abridge access to library resources, including library-initiated programs, based on an individual's economic background or ability to pay.

Adopted January 27, 1982, by the ALA Council; amended June 26, 1990; July 12, 2000.

http://ifmanual.org/libraryinitiated

CHAPTER 5

Challenges

A n incident . . . a Challenge . . . CENSORSHIP!!
Despite the training, the reading, and the hard work to build collections that reflect the community's needs, formal complaints cause a librarian's heart to drop into her sensible shoes. My advice:

- Take a deep breath—take four or five of them
- Eat chocolate
- Notify the library board and mayor
- Eat more chocolate

After these steps, blood pressure returns to normal, and rational thought is possible again. Your librarian isn't really likely to have purchased filth and child pornography—the user is obviously upset, but the staff member must remain calm, professional, and sympathetic, if not to the user's reasons for attacking the target, at least to her emotional state and constitutional right. As I said in an earlier chapter, the library's policies and procedures are written for moments like this, and the librarian's job is to follow them. Anyone who hopes to avoid a nasty mess by simply "disappearing" the item may be faced with an expensive lawsuit for taking an action based on "improper motivation."

It's my experience in a major controversy that the librarian is facing three "rings" of people:

- In the ring closest to her are those who are committed to having the library get rid of the item at issue—they will never be the library's friend (for a variety of reasons), and she's not talking to those people.
- In the ring farthest from her are those who are committed to having the library keep the item at issue—they will always be the library's friend, and she's not talking to those people.
- In the middle, the largest ring of the three, are those who haven't yet formed an opinion about the item at issue—they can be educated and persuaded by an articulate, professional approach, and the librarian is talking to those people.

It's also been my experience that about 90 percent of the requests for reconsideration that appear at the reference desk also end there—once the librarian explains the role of the library in a democracy, the person recognizes that the library serves the entire community and leaves with no intention of filing a formal complaint. I believe our success rate is so high because the librarian understands the "petition" part of the First Amendment as well as the "freedom of speech," and she treats the user with the respect owed to someone exercising his or her constitutional rights.

In fact, a formal request for reconsideration may involve as many as four constitutional rights:

"Congress shall make no law . . . abridging the freedom of speech . . . or the right of the people . . . to petition the Government for a redress of grievances." (First Amendment)

"The right of the people to be secure in their persons, houses, papers, and effects, against unreasonable searches and seizures, shall not be violated . . ." (Fourth)

"No person shall . . . be deprived of life, liberty, or property, without due process of law . . ." (Fifth)

". . . Nor shall any State . . . deny to any person within its jurisdiction the equal protection of the laws." (Fourteenth)

Libraries: An American Value

Libraries in America are cornerstones of the communities they serve. Free access to the books, ideas, resources, and information in America's libraries is imperative for education, employment, enjoyment, and self-government. Libraries are a legacy to each generation, offering the heritage of the past and the promise of the future. To ensure that libraries flourish and have the freedom to promote and protect the public good in the twenty-first century, we believe certain principles must be guaranteed.

To that end, we affirm this contract with the people we serve:

   We defend the constitutional rights of all individuals, including children and teenagers, to use the library's resources and services;

   We value our nation's diversity and strive to reflect that diversity by providing a full spectrum of resources and services to the communities we serve;

   We affirm the responsibility and the right of all parents and guardians to guide their own children's use of the library and its resources and services;

   We connect people and ideas by helping each person select from and effectively use the library's resources;

   We protect each individual's privacy and confidentiality in the use of library resources and services;

   We protect the rights of individuals to express their opinions about library resources and services;

   We celebrate and preserve our democratic society by making available the widest possible range of viewpoints, opinions and ideas, so that all individuals have the opportunity to become lifelong learners—informed, literate, educated, and culturally enriched.

Change is constant, but these principles transcend change and endure in a dynamic technological, social, and political environment.

By embracing these principles, libraries in the United States can contribute to a future that values and protects freedom of speech in a world that celebrates both our similarities and our differences, respects individuals and their beliefs, and holds all persons truly equal and free.

Adopted February 3, 1999, by the Council of the American Library Association.

http://ifmanual.org/americanvalue

Because this aspect of dealing with the public is so fraught with potential problems, former ALA president Ann Symons asked a committee to write a policy document that tells users what they should expect the library to do for them, as opposed to the Library Bill of Rights, which is directed to libraries and librarians. That document is Libraries: An American Value.

To help the library community understand this new policy, I wrote the article "Libraries: A Misunderstood American Value," which appeared in *American Libraries*.[1] The first part of this article addresses why people are inclined to file requests for reconsideration:

> Every challenge to a book, video or magazine in a library inevitably raises the question, "Why? What is there about this item that causes someone to request formally that it be denied to everyone in the community?" On its surface, the complaint frequently cites profane language, religious beliefs, or sex and claims to want to protect minors from objectionable content. The underlying reason, however, often rests on misconceptions about the role of a library in a democracy.
>
> Those of us who have dealt with challenges will recognize these or similar comments:
>
> - "Libraries should have only good books on their shelves."
> - "Everyone agrees this video is trash."
> - "The library only has one book expressing one (my) viewpoint and four that oppose it; therefore, the library is biased."
> - "The library won't listen to my complaint."
> - "Why can my children check out an R-rated video from the library when they can't see the same film in a theater?"
>
> All these comments represent faulty assumptions that reflect a combination of human nature and basic misunderstandings about libraries. For example, people believe we endorse the content of the items in our collections because we only buy "good books." If we're fulfilling our obligation to our communities, however, we're buying titles that present differing viewpoints on as many issues as possible and can't logically endorse all of them. The definition of "good" depends, of course, on the reader's beliefs, and those who find something offensive may feel betrayed by a librarian they assumed to hold those same beliefs.
>
> In another aspect of this example, people feel most comfortable associating with others who share their beliefs and values. When users claim that "everyone agrees . . . ," they're talking about only those people in the community they know. However, it doesn't take long behind a reference desk to understand just how diverse our communities really are, and we have an obligation to represent all members of the community, not just those whose views represent a large group, or even a majority.

While we strive to provide diverse viewpoints, people may misunderstand the definition of "represent," particularly if they assume it means an equal number of items for different sides of an issue. Often an equal number of titles simply hasn't been published, or perhaps the information was distributed only as a flyer at the county fair. In some extreme cases, the publisher or producer may refuse to sell to any agency of government, including libraries. Access to the Internet has greatly increased our ability to provide material not available through more traditional means, but even with this access, representation may not necessarily mean equal numbers of opposing views.

The reconsideration procedure is another area that can cause confusion. If users repeatedly see their requests to remove material denied, they think we're not taking those requests seriously and discount the entire process. People assume that if we don't agree with them, we're acting on our personal beliefs rather than objectively considering the work and the needs of the entire community, and applying a procedure adopted by the library board.

Judging by the number of complaints dealing with material available to children, the biggest problems occur when parents don't understand our role in serving children. First, they assume we won't have books they find offensive in our collections, or, if we do, that we will make the same decisions about what their children are allowed to check out that they would. They also don't understand that the library, as an agency of government, has to follow different rules about restricting access to information than a private business.[2]

There is no guarantee that your library will not face a prolonged, difficult, and sometimes irrational incident about something on the shelves, on the monitor, or in the meeting room, regardless of the library's preparation. The response, however, needs to be established in advance of a problem, and the staff needs to be trained and ready to respond to those users who want to "petition the Government for a redress of grievances." Sample forms and response letters to consider are shown on the following pages.

CASE STUDY 1

Martha looked at the application from the local Right to Life chapter for exhibit space in the main display case and then at the display itself. Despite the complaints the library had already received, she saw nothing that didn't meet the library policy's requirements. The night after the Selection Committee voted to keep the display as it was, the director had departed for a preplanned, month-long trip to Italy, and he'd

Sample Request for Reconsideration of Library Resources

[This is where you identify who, in your own structure, has authorized use of this form—Director, Board of Trustees, Board of Education, etc.—and to whom to return the form.]

Example: The Library Board of Mainstream County, U.S.A., has delegated the responsibility for selection and evaluation of library resources to the Library director and designated staff, and it has established reconsideration procedures to address concerns about those resources. Completion of this form is the first step in those procedures. If you wish to request reconsideration of library resources or programs, please return the completed form to the Library Director, Mainstream Public Library, Mainstream Plaza, Anytown, U.S.A.

Name _____

Address _____

City _____ State _____ Zip _____

Phone _____ Date _____

Do you represent self? _____ Organization? _____

Resource on which you are commenting:

_____ Book _____ Textbook _____ Video _____ Display _____ Magazine _____ Library Program

_____ Audio Recording _____ Newspaper _____ Electronic Information/Network

_____ Other *(please specify)* _____

_____

Title _____

Author/Producer _____

What brought this resource to your attention?

Have you examined the entire resource?

What concerns you about the resource? *(use other side or additional pages if necessary)*

Are there resource(s) you suggest to provide additional information and/or other viewpoints on this topic?

left her in charge. Now Martha had to handle the staff, the media, the angry folks who might or might not actually use the library, and the library stalwarts. She'd also seen a number of reconsideration forms from users clearly outside the library's juris-diction, but nothing in the policies addressed that problem. There had also been a growing number of downright nasty phone calls and e-mail messages—anonymous, of course. She decided it was time to call an all-staff meeting, to arrange for 24/7 armed protection, and to find a place for the hearing that would hold the number of people she expected and that wouldn't break the library's budget—assuming there was a budget line that would cover this situation. Just after she talked to the mayor's administrative assistant, she learned that the library was being picketed by those who wanted the display to disappear, while being counter-picketed by those who wanted the display to remain.

Martha certainly has a difficult problem. With any luck, her director will have introduced her to the library board members, the mayor, and the county assem-bly, so she's not a complete unknown if she has to represent the library at a re-consideration—or budget—hearing.

Even if the library's policies are in place, there are important details about implementing them that each staff member who might be in charge needs to know:

- Does the library respond to complaints outside of the community it serves?
- Is it possible to hold a public hearing about a reconsideration outside the library? If so, who reserves the venue and who pays for it?
- Does the county have a media relations person to handle the press and other media? If so, can the librarian-in-charge handle inquiries, or must she pass all of them to the county person?
- Does the librarian present the library's case in a public hearing? If so, does the county attorney work with the librarian to prepare her testimony?
- Can the librarian request increased police coverage?

Of these points, I think the most important is the collaboration between the librarian and the county attorney. Regardless of the person who represents the library, the testimony lays the legal groundwork. If the library doesn't make its case at the initial hearing, it may have problems in the future if the matter goes to court.

There are also important details to consider about the hearing itself:

- Does the county have or will it hire a hearing officer?
- Who will establish and/or track the time limits for speakers?

Sample Letter in Response to a Complaint

Dear _____,

    Thank you for taking the time to share your concerns about _____ and for your participation in your child's reading choices.

    As a result of your request, the Selection Committee, which is composed of all the professional staff, gathered reviews, read the book, and discussed whether or not this particular book met the selection criteria established for the library by the Library Board. We decided the book does meet those criteria for its intended audience, and we voted to keep it in the collection where it is.

    I have attached a copy of the Collection Development Policy with the selection criteria for your convenience. I have also attached the reviews that appeared about this book in the professional and children's literature journals we consult.

    As I'm sure you understand, the library serves the needs of the entire community, and we have an obligation to provide materials that reflect an extremely wide range of viewpoints and beliefs. While not every book is right for every reader, we are confident that there are books in the collection that you will find appropriate for yourself and your family.

    If you'd like help locating something that meets your needs, please let us know. There's always someone available at the Reference Desk and in the Children's Room who can show you how to find material you'll enjoy.

    Please let me know if you have any questions or would like to discuss your concerns further.

Sincerely,

- Who can authorize police coverage for the hearing?
- Who decides whether the library board will announce its decision at the end of the hearing or at a subsequent meeting?

As a witness to a twelve-hour school board meeting to decide whether or not to retain *Way of Love, Way of Life: A Young Person's Introduction to What It Means to Be Gay*, I heartily recommend establishing time limits for each speaker and for the hearing itself. Those who are not able to deliver spoken testimony can always send in written comments by a date established by the hearing officer or other official.

In any major incident, emotions run high, and there may be difficult confrontations with users. Anyone who is in charge of a library should not hesitate to reassure the staff about their safety and to call for a police presence if necessary. On the other hand, *dealing with confrontations, sometimes unpleasant, is part of the job. Librarians should not back away from adding potentially controversial material to their collections because they do not want to deal with confrontation.*

The photo below is from the *Fairbanks Daily News-Miner*,[3] taken when the library was picketed and counter-picketed in the course of a major incident. It's my favorite library photograph because it so clearly illustrates the First Amendment rights to freedom of speech and to petition for redress of grievance.

Challenged Materials
An Interpretation of the Library Bill of Rights

Libraries: An American Value states, "We protect the rights of individuals to express their opinions about library resources and services." The American Library Association declares as a matter of firm principle that it is the responsibility of every library to have a clearly defined written policy for collection development that includes a procedure for review of challenged materials. Selection of online resources, including Web sites, should also be governed by this collection development policy and be subject to the same procedures for review of challenged materials. This policy reflects the Library Bill of Rights and is approved by the appropriate governing authority.

Challenged materials should remain in the collection during the review process. The Library Bill of Rights states in Article I that "Materials should not be excluded because of the origin, background, or views of those contributing to their creation," and in Article II, that "Materials should not be proscribed or removed because of partisan or doctrinal disapproval." Freedom of expression is protected by the Constitution of the United States, but constitutionally protected expression is often separated from unprotected expression only by a dim and uncertain line. The Supreme Court has held that the Constitution requires a procedure designed to examine critically all challenged expression before it can be suppressed.[1] A hearing is a part of this procedure. Materials that meet the criteria for selection and inclusion within the collection should not be removed.

Therefore, any attempt, be it legal or extra-legal,* to regulate or suppress materials in libraries must be closely scrutinized to the end that protected expression is not abridged.

Notes

1. *Bantam Books, Inc. v. Sullivan,* 372 U.S. 58 (1963).

* "Extra-legal" refers to actions that are not regulated or sanctioned by law. These can include attempts to remove or suppress materials by library staff and library board members that circumvent the library's collection development policy, or actions taken by elected officials or library board members outside the established legal process for making legislative or board decisions. "Legal process" includes challenges to library materials initiated and conducted pursuant to the library's collection development policy, actions taken by legislative bodies or library boards during official sessions or meetings, or litigation undertaken in courts of law with jurisdiction over the library and the library's governing body.

Adopted June 25, 1971; amended July 1, 1981; amended January 10, 1990; January 28, 2009, by the ALA Council.

http://ifmanual.org/challengedmaterials

QUESTIONS TO ASK

The wonderful list below is from the New York Library Association:

Has your library ever . . .

- Not purchased material because a review or publisher's catalog indicated that it was for "mature readers," had explicit language or illustrations, or might be controversial?
- Not purchased a popular book because it might be unpopular with parents or pressure groups in the community?
- Not purchased material because of the origin, background, or views of the author?
- Not purchased sex instruction materials from a conservative religious point of view because a staff member found them to be personally offensive?
- Not purchased magazines, videos, rock or rap music, or books because "they are so popular they might be stolen"?
- Not purchased material concerning minorities because "no one in our community is like that"?
- Not purchased a popular recording because of controversial lyrics or cover art?
- Purchased a potentially controversial book, but put it in the adult collection rather than the young adult collection for which it was intended?
- Reviewed a potentially controversial item and recommended that it not be purchased because of lack of literary merit, even though other non-controversial materials in the collection also lacked literary merit?
- Checked a magazine for potentially controversial content, language, or illustrations, and then restricted access or removed it from the collection?
- Labeled controversial materials in order to "warn" or prejudice possible users?
- Restricted children's use of certain sections of the library (e.g., adult reading room), types of materials (e.g., videos), or services (e.g., interlibrary loan)?
- Placed potentially controversial materials in restricted areas so that patrons are required to request them?
- Denied library use to someone because of his or her age, gender, sexual orientation, ethnicity, or political or religious views?
- Set policies based on video or music producers' ratings to restrict access even though local ordinances don't prohibit use by minors?
- Responded to a challenge and removed objectionable material without going through a formal reconsideration of materials process?
- Cooperated in violating the right to privacy of your users by providing unauthorized access to their library records?
- Prohibited use of your meeting room or bulletin board to groups whose views you disagreed with?

If you answered yes to any of these questions, it's time to review your intellectual freedom practices![4]

One point I would add to the list—Am I overreacting?

NOTES

1. June Pinnell-Stephens, "Libraries: A Misunderstood American Value," *American Libraries* 30, no. 6 (June/July 1999): 76–78+.
2. Ibid., 76–78+.
3. *Fairbanks Daily News-Miner,* October 11, 1995, p. 1.
4. New York Library Association website.

CHAPTER 6

Privacy and Confidentiality

The many facets of privacy and confidentiality include everything from whether or not to reveal the titles a child has checked out to a parent, to handling a National Security Letter from the FBI. The place to start is the definitions, and these excerpts from "Privacy: An Interpretation of the Library Bill of Rights" answer one of the first questions: "What's the difference between confidentiality and privacy?"

> In a library (physical or virtual), the right to privacy is the right to open inquiry without having the subject of one's interest examined or scrutinized by others. Confidentiality exists when a library is in possession of personally identifiable information about users and keeps that information private on their behalf.

The condensed answer is that confidentiality is concerned with information that the library controls, while privacy relies on both the user and the library cooperating to protect privacy rights.

The basis for library concern lies in the Fourth Amendment to the U.S. Constitution:

> The right of the people to be secure in their persons, houses, papers, and effects, against unreasonable searches and seizures, shall not be violated, and no Warrant shall issue, but upon probable cause, supported by Oath or affirmation, and particularly describing the place to be searched, and persons or things to be seized.

Under the Fourth Amendment, the government cannot snoop into a person's "papers and effects" without a court order, issued after the government or law enforcement has argued that it has a very good reason to look for a specific piece of information that it believes is held in a specific place. A problem that sometimes surfaces is that "privacy" appears nowhere as a specific right. It is, instead, an "implied" or "derived" right.

There is a U.S. statute that protects a user's privacy in one limited circumstance, a law that protects the privacy of someone who rents a video from a commercial video store. It was passed after the confirmation hearings of Judge Robert Bork, when some of those opposed to elevating him to the Supreme Court publicized his video rentals. During the debate, the ALA tried to add library records to that law, but the FBI fought against including them. It had been conducting the "Library Awareness" program, trying to enlist librarians to tell them what resources users from cold war enemies were consulting, and didn't want to have the program shut down.

Fortunately, forty-eight states and the District of Columbia have statutes that now protect the information about the material that users check out, essentially, the records that join the user with the content they want. The remaining two states have opinions from their attorneys general that produce the same effect. Additionally, some states also have an explicit right to privacy in their constitutions, which clarifies the level of protection and scrutiny that will be accorded to library records.

The Alaska Constitution clearly guarantees the right to privacy; however, it's up to the legislature to "implement this section," and there are no guidelines. Other states have either more or less explicit guarantees, or none at all, and each library has to be aware of the ramifications of its state's laws.

In Alaska, the confidentiality statute is an exception to the public records provisions. In other states, the authority may be an explicit guarantee of privacy for library records, and, again, the library must be aware of the statutory requirements. Because there are so many variables from state to state, every library must carefully develop its policies in view of federal and state law.

Samples from State Constitutions
CONSTITUTIONAL RIGHTS

The earlier state constitutions relied on the "search and seizure" right from the federal constitution as their model. Later, mostly western, states began using an explicit right to privacy instead of the earlier implied right.

Alaska State Constitution

Section 1.22—Right of Privacy

The right of the people to privacy is recognized and shall not be infringed. The legislature shall implement this section. (Approved August 22, 1972)
[The Alaska Constitution clearly guarantees the right to privacy; however, it's up to the legislature to "implement this section," and there are no guidelines.]

Pennsylvania State Constitution

Section 8: Security from Searches and Seizures

The people shall be secure in their persons, houses, papers and possessions from unreasonable searches and seizures, and no warrant to search any place or to seize any person or things shall issue without describing them as nearly as may be, nor without probable cause, supported by oath or affirmation subscribed by the affiant. (Approved 1776)

Kansas State Constitution

Section 15: Search and Seizure

The right of the people to be secure in their persons and property against unreasonable searches and seizures shall be inviolate; and no warrant shall issue but on probable cause, supported by oath or affirmation, particularly describing the place to be searched and the persons or property to be seized. (Approved 1859)

Washington State Constitution

Section 7. Invasion of Private Affairs or Home Prohibited

No person shall be disturbed in his private affairs, or his home invaded, without authority of law. (Approved 1889)

Sample Library Confidentiality Statutes

Alaska Stat. § 40.25.140 Confidentiality of library records

(a) Except as provided in (b) of this section, the names, addresses, or other personal identifying information of people who have used materials made available to the public by a library shall be kept confidential, except upon court order, and are not subject to inspection under AS 40.25.110 or 40.25.120. This section applies to libraries operated by the state, a municipality, or a public school, including the University of Alaska.

(b) Records of a public elementary or secondary school library identifying a minor child shall be made available on request to a parent or guardian of that child.

Illinois Library Records Confidentiality Act, 75 ILCS 70/1

Sec. 1. (a) The registration and circulation records of a library are confidential information. No person shall publish or make any information contained in such records available to the public unless:

(1) required to do so under a court order; or

(2) the information is requested by a sworn law enforcement officer who represents that it is impractical to secure a court order as a result of an emergency where the law enforcement officer has probable cause to believe that there is an imminent danger of physical harm. The information requested must be limited to identifying a suspect, witness, or victim of a crime. The information requested without a court order may not include the disclosure of registration or circulation records that would indicate materials borrowed, resources reviewed, or services used at the library. If requested to do so by the library, the requesting law enforcement officer must sign a form acknowledging the receipt of the information. A library providing the information may seek subsequent judicial review to assess compliance with this Section.

This subsection shall not alter any right to challenge the use or dissemination of patron information that is otherwise permitted by law.

(b) This Section does not prevent a library from publishing or making available to the public reasonable statistical reports regarding library registration and book circulation where those reports are presented so that no individual is identified therein.

(b-5) Nothing in this Section shall be construed as a privacy violation or a breach of confidentiality if a library provides information to a law enforcement officer under item (2) of subsection (a).

(c) For the purpose of this Section,

(i) "library" means any public library or library of an educational, historical or eleemosynary institution, organization or society;

(ii) "registration records" includes any information a library requires a person to provide in order for that person to become eligible to borrow books and other materials and

(iii) "circulation records" includes all information identifying the individual borrowing particular books or materials.

Library Confidentiality Statutes

Both Congress and state legislatures may enact specific statutes that recognize or extend privacy rights. Forty-eight states and the District of Columbia have adopted laws that specifically recognize the confidentiality of library records.

The substance of these statutes differs from state to state. Most declare library circulation records to be confidential and not subject to disclosure under the state's open records law or Freedom of Information Act. Many states choose to extend additional protection to library records by imposing a duty on the library to protect user records from disclosure, and limiting the circumstances under which a library may release records to third parties or law enforcement officers. For example, many state library confidentiality laws require service of a court order before a library can disclose records to law enforcement officers.

Library confidentiality laws may not apply to every library in a state, or may except some users from full coverage of the law. For example, some state laws do not apply to private libraries, or exclude school libraries and academic libraries. A few state laws contain exceptions that permit parents of minor children to examine their children's library records. Other states choose to protect the confidentiality of all library users' records, without regard to the status of the library user, or the funding, ownership, or control of the library.

State library confidentiality laws should be recognized and included in library policy whenever they are applicable to the library and its users. Library confidentiality laws serve as public policy exemplars that provide a rationale and basis for the library's written policies protecting the confidentiality of library records.

Additional Resources

State Privacy Laws Regarding Library Records (available online at www.ala.org/oif/stateprivacylaws)

In every jurisdiction, the library must write a policy that incorporates the following critical aspects of library use from "Privacy: An Interpretation of the Library Bill of Rights":

> When users recognize or fear that their privacy or confidentiality is compromised, true freedom of inquiry no longer exists.
>
> . . . Lack of privacy and condientiality has a chilling effect on users' choices.
>
> . . . Users have the right to use a library without any abridgement of privacy that may result from equating the subject of their inquiry with behavior.

I think these two sentences distill the concerns that most users have about privacy in the library:

- If a user doesn't trust the library to protect his records, he'll stop using the library, which is the "chilling effect"; and
- If a user thinks someone is trying to predict what she'll do on the basis of what she checks out of the library, she'll stop using the library, again, the "chilling effect."

The last point demonstrates how important it is for libraries to be vigilant about confidentiality. If it were truly possible to predict behavior based on a reader's preferred reading material, the population would have been decimated years ago, based on the popularity of murder mysteries.

CASE STUDY 1

Tiffany was So Embarrassed. When her mother picked her up after school, in front of Debra and Caitlin, her mother said she'd been to the public library and had to pay a bundle in overdue fines, so she had asked about items that were close to their due dates. Her mother asked Tiff where the books were about lesbian relationships that she'd checked out, because Tiff's mom was going to return them because they were just about due. It's not like Tiff's a lesbian—she was just curious and wanted to find out about it. Now what was she going to say to her friends?

An example like this illustrates how important it is to protect confidentiality for library users, regardless of age. Libraries need to check their states' laws about confidentiality of library records and craft their policies and procedures to conform to them. In this case, the records of a minor have been released to her parent, which could be a violation of the confidentiality statute in many states.

Privacy
An Interpretation of the Library Bill of Rights

Privacy is essential to the exercise of free speech, free thought, and free association. The courts have established a First Amendment right to receive information in a publicly funded library.[1] Further, the courts have upheld the right to privacy based on the Bill of Rights of the U.S. Constitution.[2] Many states provide guarantees of privacy in their constitutions and statute law.[3] Numerous decisions in case law have defined and extended rights to privacy.[4]

In a library (physical or virtual), the right to privacy is the right to open inquiry without having the subject of one's interest examined or scrutinized by others. Confidentiality exists when a library is in possession of personally identifiable information about users and keeps that information private on their behalf.[5]

Protecting user privacy and confidentiality has long been an integral part of the mission of libraries. The ALA has affirmed a right to privacy since 1939.[6] Existing ALA policies affirm that confidentiality is crucial to freedom of inquiry.[7] Rights to privacy and confidentiality also are implicit in the Library Bill of Rights'[8] guarantee of free access to library resources for all users.

Rights of Library Users

The Library Bill of Rights affirms the ethical imperative to provide unrestricted access to information and to guard against impediments to open inquiry. Article IV states: "Libraries should cooperate with all persons and groups concerned with resisting abridgement of free expression and free access to ideas." When users recognize or fear that their privacy or confidentiality is compromised, true freedom of inquiry no longer exists.

In all areas of librarianship, best practice leaves the user in control of as many choices as possible. These include decisions about the selection of, access to, and use of information. Lack of privacy and confidentiality has a chilling effect on users' choices. All users have a right to be free from any unreasonable intrusion into or surveillance of their lawful library use.

Users have the right to be informed what policies and procedures govern the amount and retention of personally identifiable information, why that information is necessary for the library, and what the user can do to maintain his or her privacy. Library users expect and in many places have a legal right to have their information protected and kept private and confidential by anyone with direct or indirect access to that information. In addition, Article V of the Library Bill of Rights states: "A person's right to use a library should not be denied or abridged because of origin, age, background, or views." This article precludes the use of profiling as a basis for any breach of privacy rights. Users have the right to use a library without any abridgement of privacy that may result from equating the subject of their inquiry with behavior.[9]

Responsibilities in Libraries

The library profession has a long-standing commitment to an ethic of facilitating, not monitoring, access to information. This commitment is implemented locally through development, adoption, and adherence to privacy policies that are consistent with applicable federal, state, and local law. Everyone (paid or unpaid) who provides governance, administration, or service in libraries has a responsibility to maintain an environment respectful and protective of the privacy of all users. Users have the responsibility to respect each others' privacy.

For administrative purposes, librarians may establish appropriate time, place, and manner restrictions on the use of library resources.[10] In keeping with this principle, the collection of personally identifiable information should only be a matter of routine or policy when necessary for the fulfillment of the mission of the library. Regardless of the technology used, everyone who collects or accesses personally identifiable information in any format has a legal and ethical obligation to protect confidentiality.

Conclusion

The American Library Association affirms that rights of privacy are necessary for intellectual freedom and are fundamental to the ethics and practice of librarianship.

Notes

1. Court opinions establishing a right to receive information in a public library include *Board of Education. v. Pico,* 457 U.S. 853 (1982); *Kreimer v. Bureau of Police for the Town of Morristown,* 958 F.2d 1242 (3d Cir. 1992); and *Reno v. American Civil Liberties Union,* 117 S.Ct. 2329, 138 L.Ed.2d 874 (1997).

2. See in particular the Fourth Amendment's guarantee of "the right of the people to be secure in their persons, houses, papers, and effects, against unreasonable searches and seizures," the Fifth Amendment's guarantee against self-incrimination, and the Ninth Amendment's guarantee that "the enumeration in the Constitution, of certain rights, shall not be construed to deny or disparage others retained by the people." This right is explicit in Article Twelve of the Universal Declaration of Human Rights: "No one shall be subjected to arbitrary interference with his privacy, family, home or correspondence, nor to attacks upon his honour and reputation. Everyone has the right to the protection of the law against such interference or attacks." See: http://www.un.org/Overview/rights.html. This right has further been explicitly codified as Article Seventeen of the "International Covenant on Civil and Political Rights," a legally binding international human rights agreement ratified by the United States on June 8, 1992. See http://www.unhchr.ch/html/menu3/b/a_ccpr.htm.

3. Ten state constitutions guarantee a right of privacy or bar unreasonable intrusions into citizens' privacy. Forty-eight states protect the confidentiality of library users' records by law, and the attorneys general in the remaining two states have issued opinions recognizing the privacy of users' library records. See "State Privacy Laws," http://ala.org/ala/aboutala/offices/oif/ifgroups/stateifcchairs/stateifcinaction/stateprivacy.cfm.

4. Cases recognizing a right to privacy include *NAACP v. Alabama,* 357 U.S. 449 (1958); *Griswold v. Connecticut,* 381 U.S. 479 (1965); *Katz v. United States,* 389 U.S. 347 (1967); and *Stanley v. Georgia,* 394 U.S. 557 (1969). Congress recognized the right to privacy in the Privacy Act of 1974 and Amendments (5 U.S.C. Sec. 552a), which addresses the potential for government's violation of privacy through its collection of personal information. The Privacy Act's "Congressional Findings and Statement of Purpose" state in part: "the right to privacy is a personal and fundamental right protected by the Constitution of the United States." See http://caselaw.lp.findlaw.com/scripts/ts_search.pl?title=5&sec=552a.

5. The phrase "personally identifiable information" was established in ALA policy in 1991. See "Policy Concerning Confidentiality of Personally Identifiable Information about Library Users." Personally identifiable information can include many types of library records, for instance: information that the library requires an individual to provide in order to be eligible to use library services or borrow materials, information that identifies an individual as having

requested or obtained specific materials or materials on a particular subject, and information that is provided by an individual to assist a library staff member to answer a specific question or provide information on a particular subject. Personally identifiable information does not include information that does not identify any individual and that is retained only for the purpose of studying or evaluating the use of a library and its materials and services. Personally identifiable information does include any data that can link choices of taste, interest, or research with a specific individual.

6. Article Eleven of the Code of Ethics for Librarians (1939) asserted that "it is the librarian's obligation to treat as confidential any private information obtained through contact with library patrons." See Code of Ethics for Librarians (1939). Article Three of the current Code (2009) states: "We protect each library user's right to privacy and confidentiality with respect to information sought or received and resources consulted, borrowed, acquired, or transmitted."

7. See these ALA Policies: "Access for Children and Young People to Videotapes and Other Nonprint Formats"; "Free Access to Libraries for Minors"; Freedom to Read (http://www.ala.org/alaorg/oif/freeread.html); Libraries: An American Value; the newly revised Library Principles for a Networked World; "Policy Concerning Confidentiality of Personally Identifiable Information about Library Users"; "Policy on Confidentiality of Library Records"; "Suggested Procedures for Implementing Policy on the Confidentiality of Library Records."

8. Adopted June 18, 1948; amended February 2, 1961; and January 23, 1980; inclusion of "age" reaffirmed January 23, 1996, by the ALA Council.

9. Existing ALA Policy asserts, in part, that "the government's interest in library use reflects a dangerous and fallacious equation of what a person reads with what that person believes or how that person is likely to behave. Such a presumption can and does threaten the freedom of access to information." "Policy Concerning Confidentiality of Personally Identifiable Information about Library Users."

10. See "Guidelines for the Development and Implementation of Policies, Regulations and Procedures Affecting Access to Library Materials, Services and Facilities."

Adopted June 19, 2002, by the ALA Council.

http://ifmanual.org/privacyinterp

Unfortunately, some libraries knowingly release information to parents in violation of the state law because they don't want to deal with the consequences they expect from some members of the community.

Although Tiffany might file a complaint about how the library released her circulation records to her mother, the library could be in a difficult position if it decided to talk about the situation with the local media. Although you might urge the librarian to contact the board and mayor (or whoever the governing entities might be) in the first steps in a challenge, you might also urge her not to contact the media. Unless and until the user has filed a formal request for reconsideration, the request has been denied by the library staff, and the user has then filed an appeal to the board, the matter is purely administrative. If the library reports the incident to the media before the appeal, it may violate the state's confidentiality statute. The user may, of course, contact the media himself, and the library would then be free to respond to questions.

Just as the library needs a policy in place about selection and reconsideration, it also needs to have a policy on the books about confidentiality and privacy. Even if the library adopts "Privacy: An Interpretation of the Library Bill of Rights," it will still need to adopt a procedure to implement the policy. That implementation starts with a privacy audit to see what personal data the library is collecting, how long it's keeping the data, and how it disposes of the data, print or virtual. Instructions about conducting a privacy audit, writing a privacy policy, and developing procedures for both are available from links at www.ala.org.

Your library may be skeptical about using the already overworked staff for yet another task, but the audit can be a real eye-opener. Every department in my library was keeping some personally identifiable information (PII) it didn't need, often because "they'd always done it that way." In one case, the director assured concerned users that their unnecessary PII was shredded or deleted immediately, only to learn that the staff had continued to save the paper forms for months.

Sample Privacy Audit Form

In-House Information

Department _____

1. Does this department collect any personally identifiable information?

   Yes ___ No ___

2. If yes, please provide the following information about each element:

[Those listed below are just a few examples.]

ELEMENT	
Name:	Age:
Address:	
Phone #:	E-mail address:
ID number(s):	

WHY NEEDED	WHO HAS ACCESS	HOW LONG KEPT	HOW DISPOSED OF

Affiliated Institution

1. Does the city/university/etc. retain backup tapes of the library's databases or transactions?
2. If so, how long are the tapes retained?
3. Who has access to the tapes?
4. How are the tapes disposed of?

Vendor

1. Does the company collect personally identifiable or aggregated information about the library's users?
2. If so, who has access to the information?
3. Does the company sell this information to a third party?
4. Do library users have an opportunity to review and correct information or to opt out of any distribution of the information?

Sample Privacy Policy
STATEMENT ON PRIVACY AND CONFIDENTIALITY OF LIBRARY RECORDS
(Multnomah County, Oregon, Public Library)

I. Introduction

Multnomah County Library protects the privacy and confidentiality of all library users, no matter their age.

Oregon Revised Statute 192.502 (22) exempts from disclosure under open records law: The records of a library, including: (a) Circulation records, showing use of specific library material by a named person; (b) The name of a library patron together with the address or telephone number of the patron; and (c) The electronic mail address of a patron. Multnomah County Library's privacy and confidentiality policies are in compliance with applicable federal, state, and local laws.

Our commitment to your privacy and confidentiality has deep roots not only in the law but also in the ethics and practices of librarianship. In accordance with the American Library Association's Code of Ethics: "We protect each library user's right to privacy and confidentiality with respect to information sought or received and resources consulted, borrowed, acquired, or transmitted."

This privacy statement explains your privacy and confidentiality rights and responsibilities, the steps Multnomah County Library takes to respect and protect your privacy when you use library resources, and how we deal with personally identifiable information we collect from our users.

II. Privacy and Confidentiality Practices

Notice and Openness

We post publicly the library's privacy and information-gathering practices. Whenever practices change we notify our users.

We avoid creating unnecessary records, we avoid retaining records not needed for library business purposes, and we do not engage in practices that might place information on public view.

Information we may gather and retain about current library users includes the following:

- Information required to register for a library card or use the John Wilson special collections (e.g., name, address, telephone number, e-mail address, birthdate)

- Records of material checked out, charges owed, payments made

- Electronic access information

- Requests for interlibrary loan or reference service

- Sign-up information for library classes, programs, Sterling Room for Writers

Choice and Consent

We will not collect or retain your private and personally identifiable information without your consent. If you consent to give us your personally identifiable information, we will keep it confidential and will not sell, license or disclose personal information to any third party, except an agent working under contract to the library, without your consent, unless we are required by law to do so.

We never use or share the personally identifiable information provided to us in ways unrelated to the ones described above without also providing you an opportunity to prohibit such unrelated uses, unless we are required by law to do so.

If we make a service available for your convenience that may in some way lessen our ability to protect the privacy of your personally identifiable information or the confidentiality of information about your use of library materials and services, we will: 1.) Provide you with a privacy warning regarding that service; and 2.) Make it possible for you to "opt in" or "opt out" of that service.

User Access and Responsibility

You are entitled to view your personally identifiable information and are responsible for keeping your information accurate and up-to-date. The library will explain the process for accessing or updating your information.

Data Integrity and Security

We take reasonable steps to assure data integrity.

We protect personally identifiable information by electronically purging or manually shredding data once it is no longer needed for library business purposes.

We have invested in appropriate technology to protect the security of any personally identifiable information while it is in the library's custody.

We ensure that aggregate, summary data is stripped of personally identifiable information.

We regularly remove cookies, Web history, cached files, or other computer and Internet use records and other software code that is placed on our computers or networks.

Parents and Children

We respect the privacy and confidentiality of all library users, no matter their age. Parents or guardians of a child under age 18 who wish to obtain access to their child's library records must provide the child's library card or card number.

Items on Hold

Items placed on hold for library users are shelved by the user's last name for pick-up in public areas of our libraries. Users who do not want their holds shelved by last name may have their holds shelved by a unique user ID number (NOT the library card number).

Third Party Security

We ensure that the library's contracts, licenses, and off-site computer service arrangements reflect our policies and legal obligations concerning user privacy and confidentiality. Our agreements address appropriate restrictions on the use, aggregation, dissemination, and sale of that information, particularly information about minors.

When connecting to licensed databases outside the library, we release only information that authenticates users as registered Multnomah County Library borrowers. Nevertheless, users must be aware, when accessing remote sites, that there are limits to the privacy protection the library can provide.

Some users may choose to take advantage of RSS feeds from the library catalog, public blogs, hold and overdue notices via e-mail or text message, and similar services that send personal information related to library use via public communication networks. These users must also be aware that the library has limited ability to protect the privacy of this information once it is outside our control.

Cookies

Users accessing the library's website will need to enable cookies in order to access a number of resources available through the library. Our library servers use cookies solely to verify that a person is an authorized user in order to allow access to licensed library resources and to customize Web pages to that user's specification. Cookies sent by our library servers will disappear soon after the user's computer browser is closed.

Security Measures

Our procedures limit access to data and ensure that those individuals with access do not utilize the data for unauthorized purposes. We limit access through use of passwords and storage of data on secure servers or computers that are inaccessible from a modem or network connection.

Staff Access to Personal Data

Library staff may access personal data stored in the library's computer system only for the purpose of performing their assigned library duties. Staff will not disclose any personal data we collect from you to any other party except where required by law or to fulfill your service request. The library does not sell, lease or give users' personal information to companies, governmental agencies or individuals except as required by law or with the user's authorization.

Enforcement and Redress

If you have a question, concern, or complaint about our handling of your privacy and confidentiality rights you may file written comments with the Director of Libraries. We will respond in a timely manner and may conduct a privacy investigation or review of practices and procedures. We conduct such reviews regularly to ensure compliance with the principles outlined in this statement.

The Director of Libraries is custodian of library records and is the only party authorized to receive or comply with public records requests or inquiries from law enforcement officers. The Director may delegate this authority to designated members of the library's management team. The Director confers with the County Attorney before determining the proper response to any request for records. We will not make library records available to any agency of state, federal, or local government unless a subpoena, warrant, court order or other investigatory document is issued by a court of competent jurisdiction, showing good cause and in proper form. We have trained all library staff and volunteers to refer any law enforcement inquiries to the Office of the Director of Libraries.

Illegal Activity Prohibited and Not Protected

Users may conduct only legal activity while using library resources and services. Nothing in this statement prevents the library from exercising its right to enforce its Rules of Behavior, protect its facilities, network and equipment from harm, or prevent the use of library facilities and equipment for illegal purposes. The library can electronically monitor public computers and external access to its network and reserves the right to do so when a violation of law or library policy is suspected. Staff are authorized to take immediate action to protect the security of library users, staff, facilities, computers and the network. This includes contacting law enforcement authorities and providing information that may identify the individual(s) perpetrating a violation.

Sandra had worked for the Friends of the Library group for years, trying to raise money for an expansion of their small public library. She'd always had access to the library's user database to send out fund-raising appeals, but the new librarian wouldn't let her get the lists. It's not like she was trying to sell them life insurance or stock in a gold mine in Alaska!

This question arises when library support groups want to send out information to a natural audience—the folks who are actually interested in the library. Unless, however, the library agrees to send out information on its own, or state law allows for an exemption of some sort, the library may well be violating a confidentiality statute if it allows an outside group, even one as closely linked as a Friends group, to use its mailing list.

In cases like this, the library can send out a questionnaire to ask users if they want to allow a Friends or other library-related group to send them material, as part of an "opt in" survey. The responses from such a survey could give the library a good idea about how its users feel about privacy.

Library Records, Privacy, and the First Amendment

The right to privacy in what one reads or views in the library, and the associated right to have the records of those activities kept confidential, is founded upon the First Amendment and its protection of the right to read and receive information anonymously.

The principle that anonymity is necessary for the free exercise of First Amendment rights can be traced to the Supreme Court's recognition that the Bill of Rights protects not only the enumerated rights, but also the conditions that ensure the uninhibited exercise of those rights. Protecting the right to speak anonymously or read anonymously helps to ensure that no one is discouraged from considering or receiving controversial ideas. As the Supreme Court explained in *McIntyre v. Ohio Elections Commission,* "anonymity is a shield from the tyranny of the majority. It thus exemplifies the purpose behind the Bill of Rights and of the First Amendment in particular: to protect unpopular individuals from retaliation—and their ideas from suppression—at the hand of an intolerant society."

The Supreme Court first protected the right to read anonymously in *Lamont v. Postmaster General,* a decision that struck down as unconstitutional a law requiring individuals to identify themselves in order to receive publications that were allegedly communist propaganda. The Court's opinion relied upon the law's "chilling effect"—its potential to deter individuals from exercising their right to obtain and read controversial materials—as the grounds for overturning the law as an abridgment of First Amendment rights.

A later Supreme Court decision, *Stanley v. Georgia,* famously defended "the right to be free from state inquiry into the contents of [one's] library," when it overturned the conviction of an individual for possessing materials deemed obscene by the state of Georgia. The court rejected the state's argument that mere possession of disfavored materials justified invading the individual's privacy, asserting that "the right to be free from unwanted governmental intrusions into one's privacy is fundamental."

The result of these and similar court decisions is the recognition that the First Amendment protects the right to read and receive ideas anonymously, free from any government inquiry or interference that might chill the exercise of that right.

In particular, demands by law enforcement or the government to examine records held by a bookstore or library in order to determine what books a person has read (or what websites a person has visited) are viewed by courts as government action that can encroach upon the individual's First Amendment rights.

For example, when Independent Counsel Ken Starr issued a subpoena to two bookstores to discover the book-buying habits of Monica Lewinsky, the court found that the bookstores had proven that First Amendment interests could be harmed if the subpoena was enforced. The court ruled that, in light of the First Amendment claims made by the bookstores, the government would need to demonstrate a compelling need for the information sought and show a sufficient connection between the information sought and the grand jury investigation before the court would enforce the subpoena (*In re Grand Jury Subpoena to Kramerbooks & Afterwords, Inc.,* 26 Med. L. Rptr. 1599 (D.D.C. 1998)).

The Supreme Court of Colorado similarly quashed a search warrant served upon a local independent bookstore that sought records showing a customer's bookstore purchases. The court held that the Colorado state constitution "requires that the government, when it seeks to use a search warrant to discover customer book purchase records from an innocent, third party bookstore, must demonstrate that it has a compelling need for the information sought" and that "the court must then balance the law enforcement officials' need for the bookstore record against the harm caused to constitutional interests by execution of the search warrant" (*Tattered Cover, Inc. v. City of Thornton,* 44 P.3d 1044 (Colo. 2002)).

A local prosecutor in Decatur, Texas, served a subpoena on the local library that sought the personal information for all persons who had borrowed books on childbearing when an infant was abandoned. As in the bookstore cases, the judge applied a balancing test. He held that the subpoena represented an intrusion into library users' privacy that could only be justified when there is a compelling government objective that cannot be achieved by less intrusive means. The judge quashed the subpoena after the prosecutor could not prove the existence of a compelling need for the library records (*Decatur Public Library v. District Att'y of Wise County,* No. 90-05-192, 271st Judicial Court (Texas, 1990)).

Public libraries can ask a court to quash or set aside a subpoena or court order seeking individuals' library records if the library's administration believes producing the records will chill the exercise of the First Amendment right to read and receive information. While the First Amendment is not an absolute shield, judicial review of subpoenas will help ensure that readers' privacy is not infringed without good cause and justification.

Additional Resources

McIntyre v. Ohio Elections Commission, 514 U.S. 334 (1995)

Lamont v. Postmaster General, 381 U.S. 301, 307 (1965)

Stanley v. Georgia, 394 U.S. 557, 564 (1969)

In re Grand Jury Subpoena to Kramerbooks & Afterwords, Inc., 26 Med. L. Rptr. 1599 (D.D.C. 1998)

Tattered Cover, Inc. v. City of Thornton, 44 P.3d 1044 (Colo. 2002)

Decatur Public Library v. District Att'y of Wise County, No. 90-05-192, 271st Judicial Court (Texas, 1990)

Roberta was not happy. She'd just received a subpoena from the city police to let them snoop through her library user records on a "fishing expedition." They were asking for information about every record about every person with any transactions on February 4 and 5 last year. That request would include anyone who put a book on hold or paid their Friends of the Library dues, as well as checked out a book—hardly what she would call "particularly describing" an item, as required in the Fourth Amendment. She had a call in to her attorney and was determined to fight the order.

Good for Roberta! Unfortunately, there may not be many librarians who feel they can afford the possible bad PR if they choose to fight a subpoena, particularly when they're scrambling to keep all the funding they can in the current economic slump. It may seem obvious that the blanket subpoena was not drawn closely enough to satisfy the Fourth Amendment requirements "particularly describing . . . the things to be seized," but the police may maintain they need access to all of those records to prove their case.

It's also possible that libraries may be asked for information without a subpoena, and many staff members may be inclined to give records to the police, thinking they are behaving as "good citizens." Unfortunately, any information that is obtained without an appropriate court order may not be admitted in a trial, since it was not obtained legally. Further, the "good citizen" staff members need to understand that not only is the information useless, but the library and/or the staff members may be the targets of lawsuits themselves, because they violated their state's confidentiality law.

All libraries need to be prepared to handle a request from law enforcement, and anyone who may be in charge of the library should be able to recognize a variety of official orders and know what to do with them.

Sample Policy
HANDLING ORDERS FROM LAW ENFORCEMENT

(Fairbanks, Alaska, North Star Borough Public Library)

Outline of process that staff are expected to follow if approached by law enforcement personnel seeking information on library users and their use of library resources

All Staff

- Explain that you do not have the authority to handle the request

- Refer the officer to the Director or Librarian-in-Charge

- Do not tell anyone else that an officer has requested information

Director, Acting Director, or Librarian-in-Charge

- Try to have another staff person with you when meeting with the officer

- Ask to see the officer's identification

- Ask to see the document that describes the information sought and that authorizes its release

- If the order is a *subpoena* ("a court process compelling production of certain specific documents and other items, material and relevant to facts in issue in a pending judicial proceeding"; *Black's Law Dictionary*), other than a National Security Letter covered below, accept it and explain that you do not have the authority to release the information until the FNSB Legal Department has reviewed it. Call the Legal Department as soon as possible.

- If the order is a *search warrant* ("an order issued by a judge directing certain law enforcement officers to conduct a search of specified premises for specified things or persons, and to bring them before the court"; *Barron's Law Dictionary*):

    call the Legal Department at [phone number] during normal business hours, or the designated after-hours attorney, [name and phone number], IMMEDIATELY

    request that the officer delay execution of the warrant until a member of the Legal Department can be present, but remember that they are not obligated to wait

    if a delay is not possible, provide only the specific information described in the order

- If the *search warrant* was issued by a *Foreign Intelligence Surveillance Act (FISA) Court,* follow the instructions for search warrants above. However, a search warrant issued by a FISA court also contains a "gag order"—do not tell anyone about it except the Legal Department.

- If the order is a *National Security Letter* ("NSLs are administrative subpoenas that are issued in counterintelligence and counterterrorism investigations to obtain telephone and electronic communications records from telephone companies and Internet Service Providers"; attached FBI memo "National Security Letter Matters," 11/28/01), follow the procedures for *FISA search warrants,* including the gag order. Although these letters are not court orders, institutions are required by law to comply.

- If the officer does not have a court order or other appropriate document, take his or her name and badge number in order to report the incident to the appropriate authorities.

Neal could hardly believe what was happening. He had just received a National Security Letter from the FBI that required him to turn over all the consortium library user records for the entire month of April. Even worse, he wasn't allowed to tell anyone about it except the consortium's lawyer. Despite the "gag order," he decided to tell the rest of the consortium board members and see if they agreed to fight it. He hoped they'd agree to contact the ACLU; but in the meantime, he wished he could tell his son why he wasn't supposed to answer the phone. It all seemed too much like Orwell for him.

Whenever the library is faced with an order that involves national security, it's critical to contact its attorney immediately. Although there may be changes in the USA PATRIOT Act that address the problem for libraries, there aren't many options available until then. This situation is particularly difficult because it violates the Fourth Amendment right to privacy, as well as the First Amendment right to freedom of speech with the "gag order." Because the problem is so stressful as it's happening, it's best to be prepared beforehand by talking with the library's attorney and the staff to develop a procedure for handling the situation. One important piece of the procedure is to designate the person in charge if the director isn't available.

Thanks to the courage of the John Doe plaintiffs in the Connecticut case, there is an example for the library community to follow. Although not everyone is in a position to risk so much, both personally and professionally, there are those who will fight to protect their users' right to confidentiality and to defend their right to privacy.

For anyone who hasn't seen a National Security Letter or has questions about any other aspect of privacy in libraries, the best place to start is the "Privacy Toolkit," the "Privacy Revolution," and the "Privacy and Confidentiality" pages at www.ala.org. The information, links, and other resources can point you in the right direction.

QUESTIONS TO ASK

- Does the library have a confidentiality policy?
- Does the policy meet the requirements of the state law?
- Does the library have a privacy policy?
- Has the library conducted a privacy audit?
- Are there complaint forms to handle confidentiality/privacy issues?
- Is the staff trained to handle requests from law enforcement about library users?

Law Enforcement and Requests for Library Records

From time to time, law enforcement officers may visit the library and ask librarians or library workers to turn over records or information concerning a user's reading habits or use of the Internet. In most circumstances, however, the law does not permit either federal agents or police officers to demand an individual's library records or confidential information without first providing some form of *judicial process*—a subpoena, a search warrant, or other legally enforceable order—to the library holding the records.

- A *subpoena* is the most common means used to compel the production of library records. A subpoena is issued by a grand jury or a court and is usually signed by the prosecuting attorney; sometimes the subpoena is signed by a judge. The subpoena will identify the records that are sought for the investigation and instruct the library or librarian to produce those records at a certain date, time, and place.

  The librarian should carefully examine the subpoena with the library's legal counsel to ensure that the subpoena was issued correctly and contains all required signatures, information, and notices. If the librarian or the library's legal counsel believe that the subpoena is unjustified for any reason, or believe that compliance with the subpoena will chill the exercise of First Amendment rights in the library, the library's legal counsel can file a motion to quash the subpoena before a court with jurisdiction over the investigation.

- A *search warrant* is a court order that authorizes law enforcement officers to search for and seize particular items in a particular location. It is issued by a court and signed by a judge after a hearing to determine if "probable cause" exists—that is, good cause to believe the search will produce evidence of a crime. The police officer may serve the search warrant on the library at any time, and the library will be required to permit the search for the records or items listed in the search warrant, or provide the officer with the records or items.

  Since a search warrant authorizes the police to conduct the search without notice and without delay, there is little or no opportunity to challenge a search warrant in a court of law before the library is required to comply with the search warrant. The U.S. Supreme Court has ruled that the initial hearing to determine the existence of probable cause provides sufficient protection for individual civil rights, including First Amendment rights (*Zurcher v. Stanford Daily News,* 436 U.S. 547, 564 (1978)).

- *FISA orders* are court orders authorized by the Foreign Intelligence Surveillance Act (FISA), as amended by Section 215 of the USA PATRIOT Act. FISA orders are issued by the Foreign Intelligence Surveillance Court (FISC) and authorize FBI agents to seize "any tangible thing," including documents, records, computer disks, and any other physical object, as long as the FBI agent alleges that the item is relevant to an ongoing investigation into terrorism or foreign espionage. Under Section 215, a party served with a FISA order is subject to an automatic nondisclosure order, or "gag order," that forbids recipients of a FISA order from disclosing to anyone that they have received a FISA order, or that records have been turned over to the FBI. The USA PATRIOT Act allows the recipient of a FISA order to challenge the order in the FISA Court, but the court will not quash a FISA order unless the court finds it "unlawful." The "gag order" may be challenged in the FISA Court one year after the service of the FISA order. Libraries challenging a FISA order must consult with their attorney as soon as possible after receipt of the order.

- *National Security Letters* are specialized, written orders to turn over records that are issued by the FBI. Section 505 of the USA PATRIOT Act expanded the FBI's authority to utilize these orders to obtain certain types of records, including electronic communication records that may be held by a library providing Internet services. Like recipients of FISA orders, NSL recipients are subject to a nondisclosure order, or "gag order," forbidding any recipient from disclosing the existence of the NSL or that records were turned over to the FBI.

  The law authorizes the FBI to issue these orders without any judicial review or supervision by a court. Refusal to comply with the order or violating the nondisclosure order is a crime. A recipient of an NSL can, however, challenge the legality of an NSL and its accompanying gag order in a federal district court. Again, a library must promptly consult legal counsel if it intends to challenge the NSL.

All public libraries should have written policies and procedures for handling subpoenas, search warrants, and PATRIOT Act orders. Written policies ensure that every demand for library records and information is handled in accordance with the law and institutional policy.

Additional Resources

State Privacy Laws Regarding Library Records (http://www.ala.org/oif/stateprivacylaws)

Gotham City Model Policy 1.1 (http://www.ala.org/ala/aboutala/offices/oif/ifissues/issuesrelatedlinks/modelpolicy.cfm)

Gotham City Model Staff Directive 1.5 (http://www.ala.org/ala/aboutala/offices/oif/ifissues/issuesrelatedlinks/modelstaffdirective.cfm)

CHAPTER 7

Access to the Library: Library Management

The place to start talking about managing access to the library, from an intellectual freedom perspective, is the same list of rights from chapter 5, "Challenges":

"Congress shall make no law . . . abridging the freedom of speech . . . or the right of the people . . . to petition the Government for a redress of grievances." (First Amendment)

"The right of the people to be secure in their persons, houses, papers, and effects, against unreasonable searches and seizures, shall not be violated . . ." (Fourth)

"No person shall . . . be deprived of life, liberty, or property, without out due process of law . . ." (Fifth)

". . . Nor shall any State . . . deny to any person within its jurisdiction the equal protection of the laws." (Fourteenth)

Added to these constitutional rights are corollary rights that develop through lawsuits, or the case law. An important corollary right to free speech for libraries is the right to receive speech, since libraries have been established by government as the "quintessential locus for the receipt of information."[1] This important link has led to another corollary right to free speech, the right to use a public library.

Any case that infringes a constitutional right invokes *strict scrutiny* by the court, the highest level of judicial review.

> Under strict scrutiny, a law will be upheld *if it is necessary to achieve a compelling government purpose.* In other words, the court must regard the government's purpose as vital, as "compelling." Also, the law must be shown to be "necessary" as a means to accomplishing the end. This requires proof that the law is the least restrictive or least discriminatory alternative. If the law is not the least restrictive alternative, then it is not "necessary" to accomplish the end.
>
> Under strict scrutiny, the government has the burden of proof. That is, the law will be struck down unless the government can show that the law is necessary to accomplish a compelling government purpose. Strict scrutiny, of course, is the most intensive type of judicial review, and laws generally are declared unconstitutional when it is applied.
>
> Strict scrutiny is used when the Court evaluates discrimination based on race or national origin, generally for discrimination against aliens (although there are exceptions), and for interference with fundamental rights such as the right to vote, the right to travel, the right to privacy, and interference with freedom of speech.[2]

For libraries, the library is the government, and the policies, procedures, and regulations it adopts are the laws. Some groups who are opposed to ALA's positions claim that the Library Bill of Rights and other policies are documents of a private organization and have no standing in law, and that's true—*until the library's governing body adopts them as official policy, essentially saying that it agrees with these policies and wants them to guide the library's operations. At that point, they are official and have legal standing.*

Whether or not the library adopts ALA policies, the policies and regulations it does adopt deal with activities that can affect a number of constitutional rights.

The Right to Access Information in the Library

The First Amendment protects more than the right of free speech. It also protects other activities that are essential to the exercise of free speech that are not explicitly identified in the First Amendment. Among these is the right to receive information.

The Supreme Court first discussed the right to receive information in *Martin v. Struthers,* a 1943 decision that addressed the right to receive pamphlets from a person going door to door in a company town. In upholding the right of the town residents to receive the pamphleteer's brochures, the Court held that "the right of freedom of speech and press has broad scope . . . This freedom embraces the right to distribute literature, and necessarily protects the right to receive it." The Court's subsequent opinion in *Griswold v. Connecticut* further developed the contours of the right to receive information, identifying "the right to receive, the right to read and freedom of inquiry" among the rights protected by the First Amendment.

In 1965, Justice William Brennan elaborated on the basis for extending constitutional protection to the right to receive information:

> The protection of the Bill of Rights goes beyond the specific guarantees to protect from Congressional abridgment those equally fundamental personal rights necessary to make the express guarantees fully meaningful. I think the right to receive publications is such a fundamental right. The dissemination of ideas can accomplish nothing if otherwise willing addressees are not free to receive and consider them. It would be a barren marketplace of ideas that had only sellers and no buyers. (*Lamont v. Postmaster General,* 381 U.S. 301 (1965))

A lawsuit challenging a local school board's decision to remove several books from its high school library led to *Board of Education v. Pico,* the seminal 1982 Supreme Court opinion that explicitly recognized the right to receive information in a library. Observing that the First Amendment plays a role in protecting the public's access to discussion, debate, and the dissemination of information and ideas, the Court held that "the right to receive ideas is a necessary predicate to the recipient's meaningful exercise of his own right of speech, press and political freedom." It further identified the library as the principal locus of the freedom "to inquire, to study and to evaluate. . . ."

The analysis used in the *Pico* decision provided the foundation for another court opinion that firmly identified the public library with the right to receive information. That opinion, *Kreimer v. Bureau of Police,* did not directly concern the receipt of information; instead, it addressed the decision by a public library to ban a homeless man from the library. But in order to determine whether the library's actions were consistent with the Constitution, the Third Circuit Court of Appeals was required to decide whether or not the homeless man's expulsion implicated the First Amendment.

The Third Circuit Court of Appeals ruled that government actions that deny access to the public library do raise First Amendment concerns. In its opinion, it stated that "the First Amendment does not merely prohibit the government from enacting laws that censor information, but additionally encompasses the positive right of public access to information and ideas"; according to the court, this right necessarily includes "the right to some level of access to a public library, the quintessential locus of the receipt of information."

The constitutional framework established by the *Pico* and *Kreimer* court opinions continues to provide crucial protection for the right to receive information and the right to access information in the publicly funded library. Courts across the country have drawn upon this framework to return banned books to library shelves and to uphold principles of fair access in the library, providing direction to those responsible for developing intellectual freedom policies for libraries everywhere.

Additional Resources

Martin v. Struthers, 319 U.S. 141 (1943)

Griswold v. Connecticut, 381 U.S. 479 (1965)

Lamont v. Postmaster General, 381 U.S. 301 (1965)

Board of Education, Island Trees Union Free School District No. 26 v. Pico, 457 U.S. 853 (1982)

Kreimer v. Bureau of Police for the Town of Morristown, 958 F.2d 1242, 1259 (3d Cir. 1992)

CASE STUDY 1

Sam was surprised by the last letter he opened that day—the library had been accused of age discrimination because of the regulation that required children under ten years old to be accompanied by an adult, and federal Department of Education officials would arrive next week to discuss the issue. To the best of his knowledge, the regulation, one of several posted at the library's entrance, had never been enforced, and he couldn't even say when it had been adopted. Emily, the staff "old-timer," said she thought it was to keep children safe in a public building, and that the age was the same as the state law about child abandonment. Jeffrey, the child in the case, was a library regular, but Sam thought he was younger than ten. The incident developed after Jeffrey's father was late to pick him up, and the staff member who was trying to close the building called the police, the designated library procedure.

In this case, Sam is dealing with a regulation that is based on a valid government concern—protecting children. Even the age in the regulation is valid, as it reflects the state law related to protecting children, at least when the policy was adopted. Sam is likely hoping to negotiate with the Department of Education officials, so the library can avoid going to court. The question is whether or not this regulation is discriminatory about children's use of the library, and whether or not it's the least restrictive way of protecting them in this situation.

The case also highlights the importance of library's policies and procedures being reviewed on a regular basis by both the staff and the library board. There are often changes because of new laws, court decisions, and updates to ALA policies, and a scheduled, annual review can catch problems before they occur. It's also important to record the date of any revision, so it's possible to locate minutes from the meeting where the policy was discussed.

CASE STUDY 2

Susan had just finished her shift at the reference desk, and she'd had to kick three young men out of the library because they were looking at disgusting sites on the Internet, despite the filters—children could walk by at any time and see that filth. When she called Irene, the library director, and told her about it, Irene was not supportive, and Susan now had to meet with Irene for a "thorough review of library policy about the Internet." She was being called on the carpet for protecting children *and for stopping what amounted to sexual harassment! In fact, having to look at those sites **is** sexual harassment, and she's going to tell Irene that she's about to file a lawsuit.*

This library is looking at some very difficult issues. First, it seems to be taking on the impossible task of determining if explicit sites are obscene or merely pornographic, which may result in a lawsuit for infringing the user's right to receive speech. Second, kicking people out of the library, instead of the less restrictive option of blocking them from using the Internet for a day, may result in a lawsuit over infringing the right to use a public library.

Then there are two personnel problems. Susan seems to be ignoring the library's Internet use policy, judging by Irene's reaction, and may be facing disciplinary action, as well as putting the library at risk. As for sexual harassment because of exposure to Internet sites, so long as the library takes steps to minimize exposure by using privacy screens or recessed monitors and by enforcing time limits on Internet sessions, it should be safe from a successful lawsuit. The library should also offer guidance, like instructing the staff to turn off the monitor and reboot the computer. Recognizing that there may be incidents when a user is actually harassing the staff, the director should remind them that *the library's general regulations allow the staff to eject an actual harasser, but it's because of their behavior, not because of what they're viewing on the Internet.*

This case also highlights a critical aspect of our profession: we do not base our decisions or actions on our personal beliefs. It's quite likely that there are items in the collection, exhibits, or programs that an individual staff member finds offensive. However, every library serves a diverse public, and the library's primary purpose is to provide access to information and material for all the users it serves. The job of the librarian is to help connect the user with the information he or she wants—the librarian's beliefs have no place interfering with this transaction.

CASE STUDY 3

Donald is a newly wheelchair-bound veteran who wants to use the library for support with his online courses. Unfortunately, the stacks are so narrow and the ends so close to the walls that he can barely maneuver. Also, there are displays and chairs spread around that make his path even more difficult. He asked for help and suggested that a staff member retrieve the items he wants, but the library was short-staffed, and Donald had to wait two hours before he had his books.

Services to Persons with Disabilities
An Interpretation of the Library Bill of Rights

The American Library Association recognizes that persons with disabilities are a large and often neglected part of society. In addition to many personal challenges, some persons with disabilities face economic inequity, illiteracy, cultural isolation, and discrimination in education, employment, and the broad range of societal activities. The library plays a catalytic role in their lives by facilitating their full participation in society.

The First Amendment to the U.S. Constitution mandates the right of all persons to free expression and the corollary right to receive the constitutionally protected expression of others. A person's right to use the library should not be denied or abridged because of disabilities. The library has the responsibility to provide materials "for the interest, information, and enlightenment of all people of the community the library serves." (See also the Library Bill of Rights.) When information in libraries is not presented in formats that are accessible to all users, discriminatory barriers are created.

Library staff should be proactive in reaching out to persons with disabilities and facilitating provision of resources and services. Library staff also should be aware of the available technologies and how to assist all users with library technology. All library resources should be available in formats accessible by persons of all ages with different abilities. These materials must not be restricted by any presuppositions about information needs, interests, or capacity for understanding. The library should offer different, necessary modes of access to the same content using equipment, electronics, or software. All information resources provided directly or indirectly by the library, regardless of technology, format, or method of delivery, should be readily, equally and equitably accessible to all library users. Libraries should make every effort to support the needs of their users with disabilities and when necessary, should seek financial or other assistance to do so.

ALA recognizes that providing specialized services often requires retention of extensive patron records, such as a user's transaction histories. Libraries assume responsibility for protecting the confidentiality of all personally identifiable information entrusted to them to perform services.

Libraries should provide training opportunities for all staff and volunteers in order to sensitize them to issues affecting persons with disabilities and to teach effective techniques for providing services for users with disabilities and for working with colleagues with disabilities.

Libraries should use strategies based upon the principles of universal design to ensure that library facilities, policies, services, and resources meet the needs of all users. Libraries should provide a clear path for persons with disabilities to request accommodations that will enable them to participate fully in library programs and services. Further, libraries and schools should work with persons with disabilities, agencies, organizations, and vendors to integrate assistive technology into their facilities and services to meet the needs of persons with a broad range of disabilities, including learning, mobility, sensory, and developmental disabilities.

The preamble to the Library Bill of Rights states, "all libraries are forums for information and ideas." By removing the physical, technological, and procedural barriers

SERVICES TO PERSONS WITH DISABILITIES, continued

to accessing those forums, libraries promote the full inclusion of persons with disabilities into our society.

ALA related policy: 54.3.2 "Library Services for People with Disabilities"

Adopted January 28, 2009, by the ALA Council.

http://ifmanual.org/servicesdisabilities

Most of the problems the library will face concerning disabilities occur from omission, not commission; however, it will still need to address the restrictions faced by users with disabilities of all types. Libraries can answer some issues with software and others with equipment, but your library may have to rely on help from the staff if the building or stack arrangements won't allow physical access to the materials.

In the case of designing a new building, it is critical to work with the architects to build in full accessibility to avoid the problems libraries tend to have. Even so, there may be no option except help from the staff, and all levels of staff should receive appropriate training for all software and for sensitivity to the problems that mobility issues present.

QUESTIONS TO ASK

- Has the library's governing body formally adopted policies concerning freedom of speech and/or access to the library?
- Do the procedures implementing the policies enforce them in accordance with time/place/manner mandates?
- Does the library have a schedule of policy review?

NOTES

1. *Kreimer v. Bureau of Police for the Town of Morristown,* 958 F.2d 1242 (3d Cir. 1992).
2. Erwin Chemerinsky, *Constitutional Law: Principles and Policies* (New York: Aspen Law and Business, 1997), 416–17.

Amendments to the Constitution of the United States

Amendment I

Congress shall make no law respecting an establishment of religion, or prohibiting the free exercise thereof; or abridging the freedom of speech, or of the press; or the right of the people peaceably to assemble, and to petition the Government for a redress of grievances.

Amendment IV

The right of the people to be secure in their persons, houses, papers, and effects, against unreasonable searches and seizures, shall not be violated, and no Warrants shall issue, but upon probable cause, supported by Oath or affirmation, and particularly describing the place to be searched, and the persons or things to be seized.

Amendment V

No person shall be held to answer for a capital, or otherwise infamous crime, unless on a presentment or indictment of a Grand Jury, except in cases arising in the land or naval forces, or in the Militia, when in actual service in time of War or public danger; nor shall any person be subject for the same offence to be twice put in jeopardy of life or limb; nor shall be compelled in any criminal case to be a witness against himself, nor be deprived of life, liberty, or property, without due process of law; nor shall private property be taken for public use, without just compensation.

Amendment XIV

Passed by Congress June 13, 1866. Ratified July 9, 1868.

Note: Article I, section 2, of the Constitution was modified by section 2 of the Fourteenth Amendment.

SECTION 1.

All persons born or naturalized in the United States, and subject to the jurisdiction thereof, are citizens of the United States and of the State wherein they reside. No State shall make or enforce any law which shall abridge the privileges or immunities of citizens of the United States; nor shall any State deprive any person of life, liberty, or property, without due process of law; nor deny to any person within its jurisdiction the equal protection of the laws.

SECTION 2.

Representatives shall be apportioned among the several States according to their respective numbers, counting the whole number of persons in each State, excluding Indians not taxed. But when the right to vote at any election for the choice of electors for President and Vice-President of the United States, Representatives in Congress, the Executive and Judicial officers of a State, or the members of the Legislature thereof, is denied to any of the male inhabitants of such State, being twenty-one years of age,* and citizens of the United States, or in any way abridged, except for participation in rebellion, or other crime, the basis of representation therein shall be reduced in the proportion which the number of such male citizens shall bear to the whole number of male citizens twenty-one years of age in such State.

SECTION 3.

No person shall be a Senator or Representative in Congress, or elector of President and Vice-President, or hold any office, civil or military, under the United States, or under any State, who, having previously taken an oath, as a member of Congress, or as an officer of the United States, or as a member of any State legislature, or as an executive or judicial officer of any State, to support the Constitution of the United States, shall have engaged in insurrection or rebellion against the same, or given aid or comfort to the enemies thereof. But Congress may by a vote of two-thirds of each House, remove such disability.

SECTION 4.

The validity of the public debt of the United States, authorized by law, including debts incurred for payment of pensions and bounties for services in suppressing insurrection or rebellion, shall not be questioned. But neither the United States nor any State shall assume or pay any debt or obligation incurred in aid of insurrection or rebellion against the United States, or any claim for the loss or emancipation of any slave; but all such debts, obligations and claims shall be held illegal and void.

SECTION 5.

The Congress shall have the power to enforce, by appropriate legislation, the provisions of this article.

*Changed by section 1 of the Twenty-Sixth Amendment.

The Library Bill of Rights and Interpretations

Library Bill of Rights

The American Library Association affirms that all libraries are forums for information and ideas, and that the following basic policies should guide their services.

I. Books and other library resources should be provided for the interest, information, and enlightenment of all people of the community the library serves. Materials should not be excluded because of the origin, background, or views of those contributing to their creation.

II. Libraries should provide materials and information presenting all points of view on current and historical issues. Materials should not be proscribed or removed because of partisan or doctrinal disapproval.

III. Libraries should challenge censorship in the fulfillment of their responsibility to provide information and enlightenment.

IV. Libraries should cooperate with all persons and groups concerned with resisting abridgment of free expression and free access to ideas.

Adopted June 19, 1939, by the ALA Council; amended October 14, 1944; June 18, 1948; February 2, 1961; June 27, 1967; January 23, 1980; inclusion of "age" reaffirmed January 23, 1996.

A history of the Library Bill of Rights is found in the latest edition of the *Intellectual Freedom Manual*.

V. A person's right to use a library should not be denied or abridged because of origin, age, background, or views.

VI. Libraries that make exhibit spaces and meeting rooms available to the public they serve should make such facilities available on an equitable basis, regardless of the beliefs or affiliations of individuals or groups requesting their use.

Interpretations of the Library Bill of Rights

Although the Articles of the Library Bill of Rights are unambiguous statements of basic principles that should govern the service of all libraries, questions do arise concerning application of these principles to specific library practices.

Following are those documents designated by the Intellectual Freedom Committee as Interpretations of the Library Bill of Rights and background statements detailing the philosophy and history of each. For convenience and easy reference, the documents are presented in alphabetical order. These documents are policies of the American Library Association, having been adopted by the ALA Council.

ACCESS FOR CHILDREN AND YOUNG ADULTS TO NONPRINT MATERIALS

Library collections of nonprint materials raise a number of intellectual freedom issues, especially regarding minors. Article V of the Library Bill of Rights states, "A person's right to use a library should not be denied or abridged because of origin, age, background, or views."

ACCESS TO DIGITAL INFORMATION, SERVICES, AND NETWORKS

Freedom of expression is an inalienable human right and the foundation for self-government. Freedom of expression encompasses the freedom of speech and the corollary right to receive information. Libraries and librarians protect and promote these rights by selecting, producing, providing access to, identifying, retrieving, organizing, providing instruction in the use of, and preserving recorded expression regardless of the format or technology.

ACCESS TO LIBRARY RESOURCES AND SERVICES REGARDLESS OF SEX, GENDER IDENTITY, GENDER EXPRESSION, OR SEXUAL ORIENTATION

The American Library Association stringently and unequivocally maintains that libraries and librarians have an obligation to resist efforts that systematically exclude materials dealing with any subject matter, including sex, gender identity, or sexual orientation.

ACCESS TO RESOURCES AND SERVICES IN THE SCHOOL LIBRARY MEDIA PROGRAM

The school library media program plays a unique role in promoting intellectual freedom. It serves as a point of voluntary access to information and ideas and as a learning laboratory for students as they acquire critical thinking and problem-solving skills needed in a pluralistic society. Although the educational level and program of the school necessarily shapes the resources and services of a school library media program, the principles of the Library Bill of Rights apply equally to all libraries, including school library media programs.

CHALLENGED MATERIALS

The American Library Association declares as a matter of firm principle that it is the responsibility of every library to have a clearly defined materials selection policy in written form that reflects the Library Bill of Rights, and that is approved by the appropriate governing authority.

DIVERSITY IN COLLECTION DEVELOPMENT

Intellectual freedom, the essence of equitable library services, provides for free access to all expressions of ideas through which any and all sides of a question, cause, or movement may be explored. Toleration is meaningless without tolerance for what some may consider detestable. Librarians cannot justly permit their own preferences to limit their degree of tolerance in collection development, because freedom is indivisible.

ECONOMIC BARRIERS TO INFORMATION ACCESS

A democracy presupposes an informed citizenry. The First Amendment mandates the right of all persons to free expression, and the corollary right to receive the constitutionally protected expression of others. The publicly supported library provides free, equal, and equitable access to information for all people of the community the library serves. While the roles, goals and objectives of publicly supported libraries may differ, they share this common mission.

EVALUATING LIBRARY COLLECTIONS

The continuous review of library materials is necessary as a means of maintaining an active library collection of current interest to users. In the process, materials may be added and physically deteriorated or obsolete materials may be replaced or removed in accordance with the collection maintenance policy of a given library and the needs of the community it serves. Continued evaluation is closely related to the goals and responsibilities of all libraries and is a valuable tool of collection development. This procedure is not to be used as a convenient means to remove materials presumed to be controversial or disapproved of by segments of the community.

EXHIBIT SPACES AND BULLETIN BOARDS

Libraries often provide exhibit spaces and bulletin boards. The uses made of these spaces should conform to the Library Bill of Rights: Article I states, "Materials should not be excluded because of the origin, background, or views of those contributing to their creation." Article II states, "Materials should not be proscribed or removed because of partisan or doctrinal disapproval." Article VI maintains that exhibit space should be made available "on an equitable basis, regardless of the beliefs or affiliations of individuals or groups requesting their use."

EXPURGATION OF LIBRARY MATERIALS

Expurgating library materials is a violation of the Library Bill of Rights. Expurgation as defined by this interpretation includes any deletion, excision, alteration, editing, or obliteration of any part(s) of books or other library resources by the library, its agent, or its parent institution (if any).

FREE ACCESS TO LIBRARIES FOR MINORS

Library policies and procedures that effectively deny minors equal and equitable access to all library resources available to other users violate the Library Bill of Rights. The American Library Association opposes all attempts to restrict access to library services, materials, and facilities based on the age of library users.

IMPORTANCE OF EDUCATION TO INTELLECTUAL FREEDOM

Through education programming and instruction in information skills, libraries empower individuals to explore ideas, access and evaluate information, draw meaning from information presented in a variety of formats, develop valid conclusions, and express new ideas. Such education facilitates intellectual access to information and offers a path to intellectual freedom.

INTELLECTUAL FREEDOM PRINCIPLES FOR ACADEMIC LIBRARIES

A strong intellectual freedom perspective is critical to the development of academic library collections and services that dispassionately meet the education and research needs of a college or university community. The purpose of this statement is to outline how and where intellectual freedom principles fit into an academic library setting, thereby raising consciousness of the intellectual freedom context within which academic librarians work.

LABELING AND RATING SYSTEMS

Libraries do not advocate the ideas found in their collections or in resources accessible through the library. The presence of books and other resources in a library does not indicate endorsement of their contents by the library. Likewise, the ability for library users to access electronic information using library computers does not indicate endorsement or approval of that information by the library.

LIBRARY-INITIATED PROGRAMS AS A RESOURCE

Library-initiated programs support the mission of the library by providing users with additional opportunities for information, education, and recreation.

MEETING ROOMS

Many libraries provide meeting rooms for individuals and groups as part of a program of service. Article VI of the Library Bill of Rights states that such facilities should be made available to the public served by the given library "on an equitable basis, regardless of the beliefs or affiliations of individuals or groups requesting their use."

MINORS AND INTERNET INTERACTIVITY

The digital environment offers opportunities both for accessing information created by others and for creating and sharing new information. The rights of minors to retrieve, interact with, and create information posted on the Internet in schools and libraries are extensions of their First Amendment rights.

PRISONERS' RIGHT TO READ

The American Library Association asserts a compelling public interest in the preservation of intellectual freedom for individuals of any age held in jails, prisons, detention facilities, juvenile facilities, immigration facilities, prison work camps and segregated units within any facility.

PRIVACY

Privacy is essential to the exercise of free speech, free thought, and free association. See also "Questions and Answers on Privacy and Confidentiality."

RESTRICTED ACCESS TO LIBRARY MATERIALS

Libraries are a traditional forum for the open exchange of information. Attempts to restrict access to library materials violate the basic tenets of the Library Bill of Rights.

SERVICES TO PEOPLE WITH DISABILITIES

ALA recognizes that persons with disabilities are a large and often neglected part of society. In addition to many personal challenges, some persons with disabilities face economic inequity, illiteracy, cultural isolation, and discrimination in education, employment, and the broad range of societal activities. The library plays a catalytic role in their lives by facilitating their full participation in society.

THE UNIVERSAL RIGHT TO FREE EXPRESSION

Freedom of expression is an inalienable human right and the foundation for self-government. Freedom of expression encompasses the freedoms of speech, press, religion, assembly, and association, and the corollary right to receive information.

Code of Ethics of the American Library Association

As members of the American Library Association, we recognize the importance of codifying and making known to the profession and to the general public the ethical principles that guide the work of librarians, other professionals providing information services, library trustees and library staffs.

Ethical dilemmas occur when values are in conflict. The American Library Association Code of Ethics states the values to which we are committed, and embodies the ethical responsibilities of the profession in this changing information environment.

We significantly influence or control the selection, organization, preservation, and dissemination of information. In a political system grounded in an informed citizenry, we are members of a profession explicitly committed to intellectual freedom and the freedom of access to information. We have a special obligation to ensure the free flow of information and ideas to present and future generations.

The principles of this Code are expressed in broad statements to guide ethical decision making. These statements provide a framework; they cannot and do not dictate conduct to cover particular situations.

I. We provide the highest level of service to all library users through appropriate and usefully organized resources; equitable service policies; equitable access; and accurate, unbiased, and courteous responses to all requests.

II. We uphold the principles of intellectual freedom and resist all efforts to censor library resources.

III. We protect each library user's right to privacy and confidentiality with respect to information sought or received and resources consulted, borrowed, acquired or transmitted.

IV. We respect intellectual property rights and advocate balance between the interests of information users and rights holders.

V. We treat co-workers and other colleagues with respect, fairness, and good faith, and advocate conditions of employment that safeguard the rights and welfare of all employees of our institutions.

VI. We do not advance private interests at the expense of library users, colleagues, or our employing institutions.

VII. We distinguish between our personal convictions and professional duties and do not allow our personal beliefs to interfere with fair representation of the aims of our institutions or the provision of access to their information resources.

VIII. We strive for excellence in the profession by maintaining and enhancing our own knowledge and skills, by encouraging the professional development of co-workers, and by fostering the aspirations of potential members of the profession.

Adopted June 28, 1997, by the ALA Council; amended January 22, 2008.

The Freedom to Read Statement

The freedom to read is essential to our democracy. It is continuously under attack. Private groups and public authorities in various parts of the country are working to remove or limit access to reading materials, to censor content in schools, to label "controversial" views, to distribute lists of "objectionable" books or authors, and to purge libraries. These actions apparently rise from a view that our national tradition of free expression is no longer valid; that censorship and suppression are needed to counter threats to safety or national security, as well as to avoid the subversion of politics and the corruption of morals. We, as individuals devoted to reading and as librarians and publishers responsible for disseminating ideas, wish to assert the public interest in the preservation of the freedom to read.

Most attempts at suppression rest on a denial of the fundamental premise of democracy: that the ordinary individual, by exercising critical judgment, will select the good and reject the bad. We trust Americans to recognize propaganda and misinformation, and to make their own decisions about what they read and believe. We do not believe they are prepared to sacrifice their heritage of a free press in order to be "protected" against what others think may be bad for them. We believe they still favor free enterprise in ideas and expression.

These efforts at suppression are related to a larger pattern of pressures being brought against education, the press, art and images, films, broadcast media, and the Internet. The problem is not only one of actual censorship. The shadow of fear cast by these pressures leads, we suspect, to an even larger voluntary curtailment of expression by those who seek to avoid controversy or unwelcome scrutiny by government officials.

Such pressure toward conformity is perhaps natural to a time of accelerated change. And yet suppression is never more dangerous than in such a time of social tension. Freedom has given the United States the elasticity to endure strain. Freedom keeps open the path of novel and creative solutions, and enables change to come by choice. Every silencing of a heresy, every enforcement of an orthodoxy, diminishes the toughness and resilience of our society and leaves it the less able to deal with controversy and difference.

Now as always in our history, reading is among our greatest freedoms. The freedom to read and write is almost the only means for making generally available ideas or manners of expression that can initially command only a small audience. The written word is the natural medium for the new idea and the untried voice from which come the original contributions to social growth. It is essential to the extended discussion that serious thought requires, and to the accumulation of knowledge and ideas into organized collections.

We believe that free communication is essential to the preservation of a free society and a creative culture. We believe that these pressures toward conformity present the danger of limiting the range and variety of inquiry and expression on which our democracy and our culture depend. We believe that every American community must jealously guard the freedom to publish and to circulate, in order to preserve its own freedom to read. We believe that publishers and librarians have a profound responsibility to give validity to that freedom to read by making it possible for the readers to choose freely from a variety of offerings.

The freedom to read is guaranteed by the Constitution. Those with faith in free people will stand firm on these constitutional guarantees of essential rights and will exercise the responsibilities that accompany these rights.

We therefore affirm these propositions:

1. *It is in the public interest for publishers and librarians to make available the widest diversity of views and expressions, including those that are unorthodox, unpopular, or considered dangerous by the majority.*

   Creative thought is by definition new, and what is new is different. The bearer of every new thought is a rebel until that idea is refined and tested. Totalitarian systems attempt to maintain themselves in power by the ruthless suppression of any concept that challenges the established orthodoxy. The power of a democratic system to adapt to change is vastly strengthened by the freedom of its citizens to choose widely from among conflicting opinions offered freely to them. To stifle every nonconformist idea at birth would mark the end of the democratic process. Furthermore, only through the constant activity of weighing and selecting can the democratic mind attain the strength demanded by times like these. We need to know not only what we believe but why we believe it.

2. *Publishers, librarians, and booksellers do not need to endorse every idea or presentation they make available. It would conflict with the public interest for them to establish their own political, moral, or aesthetic views as a standard for determining what should be published or circulated.*

   Publishers and librarians serve the educational process by helping to make available knowledge and ideas required for the growth of the mind and the increase of learning. They do not foster education by imposing as mentors the patterns of their own thought. The people should have the freedom to read and consider a broader range of ideas than those that may be held by any single librarian or publisher or government or church. It is wrong that what one can read should be confined to what another thinks proper.

3. *It is contrary to the public interest for publishers or librarians to bar access to writings on the basis of the personal history or political affiliations of the author.*

   No art or literature can flourish if it is to be measured by the political views or private lives of its creators. No society of free people can flourish that draws up lists of writers to whom it will not listen, whatever they may have to say.

4. *There is no place in our society for efforts to coerce the taste of others, to confine adults to the reading matter deemed suitable for adolescents, or to inhibit the efforts of writers to achieve artistic expression.*

   To some, much of modern expression is shocking. But is not much of life itself shocking? We cut off literature at the source if we prevent writers from dealing with the stuff of life. Parents and teachers have a responsibility to prepare the young to meet the diversity of experiences in life to which they will be exposed, as they have a responsibility to help them learn to think critically for themselves. These are affirmative responsibilities, not to be discharged simply by preventing them from reading works for which they are not yet prepared. In these matters values differ, and values cannot be legislated; nor can machinery be devised that will suit the demands of one group without limiting the freedom of others.

5. *It is not in the public interest to force a reader to accept the prejudgment of a label characterizing any expression or its author as subversive or dangerous.*

The ideal of labeling presupposes the existence of individuals or groups with wisdom to determine by authority what is good or bad for others. It presupposes that individuals must be directed in making up their minds about the ideas they examine. But Americans do not need others to do their thinking for them.

6. *It is the responsibility of publishers and librarians, as guardians of the people's freedom to read, to contest encroachments upon that freedom by individuals or groups seeking to impose their own standards or tastes upon the community at large; and by the government whenever it seeks to reduce or deny public access to public information.*

It is inevitable in the give and take of the democratic process that the political, the moral, or the aesthetic concepts of an individual or group will occasionally collide with those of another individual or group. In a free society individuals are free to determine for themselves what they wish to read, and each group is free to determine what it will recommend to its freely associated members. But no group has the right to take the law into its own hands, and to impose its own concept of politics or morality upon other members of a democratic society. Freedom is no freedom if it is accorded only to the accepted and the inoffensive. Further, democratic societies are more safe, free, and creative when the free flow of public information is not restricted by governmental prerogative or self-censorship.

7. *It is the responsibility of publishers and librarians to give full meaning to the freedom to read by providing books that enrich the quality and diversity of thought and expression. By the exercise of this affirmative responsibility, they can demonstrate that the answer to a "bad" book is a good one, the answer to a "bad" idea is a good one.*

The freedom to read is of little consequence when the reader cannot obtain matter fit for that reader's purpose. What is needed is not only the absence of restraint, but the positive provision of opportunity for the people to read the best that has been thought and said. Books are the major channel by which the intellectual inheritance is handed down, and the principal means of its testing and growth. The defense of the freedom to read requires of all publishers and librarians the utmost of their faculties, and deserves of all Americans the fullest of their support.

We state these propositions neither lightly nor as easy generalizations. We here stake out a lofty claim for the value of the written word. We do so because we believe that it is possessed of enormous variety and usefulness, worthy of cherishing and keeping free. We realize that the application of these propositions may mean the dissemination of ideas and manners of expression that are repugnant to many persons. We do not state these propositions in the comfortable belief that what people read is unimportant. We believe rather that what people read is deeply important; that ideas can be dangerous; but that the suppression of ideas is fatal to a democratic society. Freedom itself is a dangerous way of life, but it is ours.

This statement was originally issued in May of 1953 by the Westchester Conference of the American Library Association and the American Book Publishers Council, which in 1970 consolidated with the American Educational Publishers Institute to become the Association of American Publishers.

Adopted June 25, 1953, by the ALA Council and the AAP Freedom to Read Committee; amended January 28, 1972; January 16, 1991; July 12, 2000; June 30, 2004.

A JOINT STATEMENT BY:
American Library Association
Association of American Publishers

SUBSEQUENTLY ENDORSED BY:
American Booksellers Foundation for Free Expression
The Association of American University Presses, Inc.
The Children's Book Council
Freedom to Read Foundation
National Association of College Stores
National Coalition Against Censorship
National Council of Teachers of English
The Thomas Jefferson Center for the Protection of Free Expression

Index

Page numbers in italic refer to case studies. Page numbers in bold refer to the text of a Library Bill of Rights (LBOR) Interpretation or ALA policy.

equity of access and right of access, 42
erasing vulgar words, *30–31*
Erznoznik v. City of Jacksonville, 25n1
"Evaluating Library Collections"
  (interpretation), **19**, 131–132
evaluation of materials
  in collection management, 16
  and decisions to discard, 18, 20
  See also materials selection
"Exhibit Spaces and Bulletin Boards"
  (interpretation), **71**, 132
exhibits and displays
  of controversial material, *66, 83, 85*
  elements of policies on, 67
  of new books and staff picks in collection
    development policy, 17
  restrictions based on content, *66,* 68–69
"Expurgation of Library Materials"
  (interpretation), **33**, 132
expurgation of materials, 30–31

F

*Faith Center Church Evangelistic Ministries, et
  al. v. Glover, et al.*, 75
FBI requests, response to, sample policy,
  110–111
Fifth Amendment
  and enforcement of Internet policy
    violations, 59
  and response to challenges, 80
  text, 125
film ratings systems, *30,* 36
filtering. *See* software filtering
First Amendment
  and privacy, 107–108
  and response to challenges, 80
  and response to National Security Letters,
    112
  and right to receive information, 117
  and software filters, 51, 57
  and tap on the shoulder enforcement of
    Internet policies, 59
  text, 125
FISA (Foreign Intelligence Surveillance Act)
  orders, 111, 113–114
formats of resources in collection development
  policy, 21–22
Fourteenth Amendment
  response to challenges, 81
  text, 126–127
Fourth Amendment
  and response to challenges, 80

and response to National Security Letters,
  112
and right of privacy, 92
text, 125
"Free Access to Libraries for Minors"
  (interpretation), **24–25**, 132
"Freedom to Read Statement," **137–141**
Friends groups and privacy of mailing lists, *106*

G

"gag order" and National Security Letters, 114
Ginsberg v. New York, 46
Griswold v. Connecticut, 117

H

harmful to minors statutes, 27, 46
hearings on complaints, preparation for, 85, 87

I

"Importance of Education to Intellectual
  Freedom" (interpretation), 132
*In re Grand Jury Subpoena to Kramerbooks &
  Afterwords, Inc.*, 107–108
indecent speech, legal definition of, 45–47
"Intellectual Freedom Principles for Academic
  Libraries," 132
intellectual freedom principles in collection
  development policy, 4, 8
*Interactive Digital Software Association v. St.
  Louis County*, 36
Internet access for non-cardholders, *61*
Internet resources, 37–62
  case study 1 (privacy protection), *48, 53*
  case study 2 (disabling filters), *53–54*
  case study 3 (tap on the shoulder), *59*
  case study 4 (content restrictions on
    minors), *60*
  case study 5 (access for non-cardholders),
    61
  popular websites, 38–39
  See also "Access to Digital Information,
    Services, and Networks"
    (interpretation)
Internet safety policies
  and blocking social networking sites, 60
  and Neighborhood Children's Internet
    Protection Act (NCIPA), 55–56
Internet Use Policy
  checklist, 61
  consequences of violations, 59
  elements, 44, 48
  sample, 50–52

processing and cataloging in collection development policy, 16
programs, complaints about, 76
public forums doctrine, 64, 65

R

reconsideration requests
in collection development policy, 8
motivations for, 82–83
responses to, 2
sample, 10, 84
religious groups and use of meeting rooms, 72, 74
Reno v. ACLU, 46
replacement materials
in collection development policy, 17
of theft-prone materials, 21
requests for reconsideration. *See* reconsideration requests
reserve items, privacy of, 103
"Restricted Access to Library Materials" (interpretation), **28–29,** 133
restrictions on access
by incomplete processing of materials, 13, 17–18
labels and ratings as, *30*
software filters in LBOR interpretation, 28
on staff-only shelving, 13, 17
and theft-prone materials, *27*
restrictions on cards for minors, *26*
review of policies, 119

S

Sable Communications of California, Inc. v. FCC, 45
sample policies. *See* policies, sample
search warrants, response to, 113–114
sample policy, 110–111
selection. *See* materials selection
"Services to Persons with Disabilities" (interpretation), **121–122,** 134
sexual harassment, *120*
social networking sites and Internet safety policies, 60
software filtering
disabling of, *53–54,* 57

and Internet use policies, 53
and right of access, 43
sample policy, 50
staff
access to users' data policy, 104
response to law enforcement requests, 110–111
training on assistance to disabled users, 123
Stanley v. Georgia, 107–108
strict scrutiny criteria, 116
subpoenas, response to, 113–114
sample policy, 110
Sund v. City of Wichita Falls, 12, 34–35

T

tap on the shoulder enforcement of policies, *59*
Tattered Cover, Inc. v. City of Thornton, 108
textbooks, collection of, 20
theft-prone materials
replacement of, 21
restrictions on access, *27*
time, place, and manner rules in public forums, 65, 66
Tinker v. Des Moines School Dist., 25n1

U

United States, et al. v. American Library Association, et al., 57, 58
"Universal Right to Free Expression, The" (interpretation), 134
user needs in collection development policy, 4

V

vendors, choice of in collection development policy, 21

W

West Virginia Bd. of Ed. v. Barnette, 25n1
wireless Internet access, sample policy for, 52
workstations, sample policy, 50–51

Z

Zurcher v. Stanford Daily News, 113